SHVETASHVATARA

UPANISHAD

Essence and Sanskrit Grammar

Ashwini Kumar Aggarwal

जय गुरुदेव

ISBN13: 978-93-92201-09-7 Paperback Edition
ISBN13: 978-93-92201-10-3 Hardbound Edition
ISBN13: 978-93-92201-15-8 Digital Edition

Title: **Shvetashvatara Upanishad**
SubTitle: **Essence and Sanskrit Grammar**

Printed and Published by
Devotees of Sri Sri Ravi Shankar Ashram
34 Sunny Enclave, Devigarh Road
Patiala 147001, Punjab, India

https://advaita56.weebly.com/
The Art of Living Centre

https://www.artofliving.org/

21st April 2021, Ram Navmi, Tara Jayanti
Punarvasu (Pushya Ashwini) Nakshatra, Vasant Ritu
Vikram Samvat 2078 Ananda, Saka Era 1943 Plava

1st Edition April 2021

जय गुरुदेव

Sri Sri Ravi Shankar

who churns the wisdom and makes it palatable

Blessing

All that you can do is to raise the level of Sattva. And then when Sattva's level is high, we have to wait one moment, any moment knowledge can dawn there.

All that you can do to have sunlight in this room, is to open the curtains and keep the windows open. And when dawn comes, it just dawns. You have the sunlight inside.

Sri Sri Ravi Shankar
A discourse on Yogasara Upanishad

Acknowledgements

A trek to far remote virgin nature reestablishes the Divine connection.

Cover Photo Credits

Dhakpo Shedrupling Monastery on bank of Beas river Kullu, inaugurated in 2005 by His Holiness the Dalai Lama. Photo by Dr. Sangeeta on trip to Rohtang Pass dated 6.June.2012

Preface

During a trek to virgin nature, the mind
stops chattering. Unbelievable things happen
to the consciousness. The body doesn't
complain. The heart feels nice and warm. And
the Lord walks in.

Veda	
Mantra Verses (Samhita)	Brahmana Verses
	Brahmana Aranyaka Upanishad

Adi Shankaracharya's masterly commentary on eleven
Upanishads is the de facto standard for Vedanta. These
eleven have been named the principal Upanishads. Though
it is said there are 1180 Upanishads written over a period of
a thousand years, actual manuscripts available as of now
are 108 only.

A chart that lists the eleven Upanishads commented on in
detail by Sankara.

Rigveda	Samaveda	Shukla Yajurveda Krishna Yajurveda	Atharvaveda
Gives the fundamental laws of creation	Gives the intrinsic harmony within creation	Gives the specific design, administrative and governing principles for a family or a nation	Gives the specific ritucharya and dinacharya for an individual

Aitareya	Kena **Chandogya**	Ishavasya **Brihadaranyaka** Katha Taittiriya Shvetashvatara	**Mandukya** Mundaka Prashna
प्रज्ञानम् ब्रह्म	तत् त्वम् असि	अहं ब्रह्म अस्मि	अयम् आत्मा ब्रह्म

Four great illuminating statements or mahavakyas are listed above with their corresponding Upanishads in **bold**.
The Shvetashvatara has its very own mahavakya -
सर्वाननशिरोग्रीवः सर्वभूतगुहाशयः । सर्वव्यापी स भगवांस्तस्मात्सर्वगतः शिवः ॥ 3.11

Vedic Sanskrit can never be adequately translated. It has sutras and dictums that can each form an entire school curriculum. The only way is to wait until words and sentences sprout after deep meditation in the presence of an enlightened master.

Yajur Veda = Yajurveda Samhita + Yajurveda Brahmana

Shvetashvatara verses are found in the Krishna Yajurveda. There is ample discussion about Brahman, the Supreme Reality, and its manifest transactional play.

Table of Contents

BLESSING 4

PREFACE..5

PRAYER...8

    Qualifications Prerequisites 9

1ST TEACHING (THE BRAINSTORMING) 9

    What is Brahman? 9
    Who has the final say?..9

2ND TEACHING (YOGIC TECHNIQUES) 34

    Surya Namaskar...34

3RD TEACHING (DEITIES OF BRAHMAN)........................46

    Who causes Sleep and Awaking?...........................46

4TH TEACHING (MANIFEST BRAHMAN) 68

    Necessity of Faith 68

5TH TEACHING (LIVING THE BRAHMAN) 96

    Transactional aspect of Brahman 96

6TH TEACHING (LEELA OF BRAHMAN) 118

    The cosmic play of Brahman 118

VERSES QUOTED IN ADI SANKARA'S BHASHYAM...........150

ETYMOLOGY OF UPANISHAD 152

LATIN TRANSLITERATION CHART............................153

VERSES FOR CHANTING 154

SANSKRIT GRAMMAR 174

CONJUGATION PROCESS OF VERB..........................177

DECLENSION PROCESS OF NOUN 178

REFERENCES 179

EPILOGUE..180

Prayer

शान्तिपाठः

ॐ सह नाववतु । सह नौ भुनक्तु । सह वीर्यं करवावहै ।
तेजस्वि नावधीतमस्तु मा विद्विषावहै ॥
ॐ शान्तिः शान्तिः शान्तिः ॥

oṃ saha nāvavatu | saha nau bhunaktu | saha vīryaṃ karavāvahai
| tejasvi nāvadhītamastu mā vidviṣāvahai ||

oṃ śānti śānti śāntiḥ ||

Peace Invocation

O Pure Loving Grace!

May we be taken care of along with our family and friends.
May we enjoy socializing and eating together.
May we support each other's vision and growth.
May our intellect be open to new ideas and changing trends.
May we spend more time in praise than abuse, may we talk
of each other's virtues rather than harp on vices.

Peace in our heart, in our body and in our environs.

श्वेताश्वतरोपनिषद् śvetāśvataropaniṣad

अथ श्वेताश्वतर–उपनिषद्

atha Shvetashvatara Upaniṣad

Now begins the Shvetashvatara

Vowel Sandhi – Guna Sandhi – अ + उ → ओ

श्वेताश्वतर + उपनिषद् →श्वेताश्वतरोपनिषद् ।

Qualifications Prerequisites

The Upanishad is a masterly text, meant for a sincere and serious aspirant. Basic qualifications include a command over language, cleanliness, and neatness in attire.

Other qualifications most essential to imbibing the knowledge are:
- Respectfulness
- Readiness to serve with cheerfulness
- Capacity to maintain discipline for a year with frugal lifestyle
- Truthfulness and candor in communication

1st Teaching (the brainstorming)

What is Brahman?

Who has the final say?

प्रथमोऽध्यायः

हरिः ॐ ब्रह्मवादिनो वदन्ति ।

किं कारणं ब्रह्म कुतः स्म जाता जीवाम केन क्व च सम्प्रतिष्ठाः ।

अधिष्ठिताः केन सुखेतरेषु वर्तामहे ब्रह्मविदो व्यवस्थाम् ॥ १

कालः स्वभावो नियतिर्यदृच्छा भूतानि योनिः पुरुष इति चिन्त्या ।

संयोग एषां न त्वात्मभावादात्माप्यनीशः सुखदुःखहेतोः ॥ २

prathamo'dhyāyaḥ

hariḥ oṃ brahmavādino vadanti | kiṃ kāraṇaṃ brahma kutaḥ sma jātā jīvāma kena kva ca sampratiṣṭhāḥ | adhiṣṭhitāḥ kena sukhetareṣu vartāmahe brahmavido vyavasthām || 1

kālaḥ svabhāvo niyatiryadṛcchā bhūtāni yoniḥ puruṣa iti cintyā | saṃyoga eṣāṃ na tvātmabhāvādātmāpyanīśaḥ sukhaduḥkhahetoḥ || 2

ब्रह्म-वादिनः Seekers of Brahman वदन्ति । brainstorm. किं So is कारणं the cause ब्रह्म Brahman? कुतः how स्म जाताः are all born? जीवामः is life supported केन how? क्व where च and सम्प्रतिष्ठाः । is the final resting place after death? अधिष्ठिताः will governs केन whose? सुखेतर-एषु laws of happiness and unhappiness. वर्तामहे we obey ब्रह्म-विदः O Knower of Brahman व्यवस्थाम् ॥ what mechanism? कालः Lord of Time स्वभावः Lord of Nature नियतिः Lord of Laws यदृच्छा Coincidence भूतानि matter योनिः form पुरुषः Self इति thus चिन्त्या । contemplate. संयोगः permutation combination एषां of these न तु or is not आत्मभावात् from emotion or genetics आत्मा Self अपि also अनीशः dependent सुख-दुःख-हेतोः ॥ happiness sorrow cause of.

1.1 Seekers of the Truth (that is deeper and more significant than that evident from sight and hearing) are having a brain storming session.

What is the meaning of Brahman? Why this creation and to what purpose? By whose will does Life get impregnated in matter? Where do we come from where do we go? What happens to us after we leave this earthly plane?

O knower of Brahman, By whose will operate the laws of Pain and pleasure that play havoc on each individual and also give solace?

1.2 Who wields most authority and has the final say? Whether wheel of Time, Seasonal changes and cyclical forces, personal necessities, one's attitude and level of understanding, pure coincidence, or the interplay of basic elements and their laws, some known, some undiscovered, some not understood.

We opine none of these listed are the real agencies, how can they be when they themselves seem so fragile, prone to error, unstable?

Nay even the innermost being inside of us is so dim that it seems to be easily overwhelmed and at a loss when faced with trying circumstances, unpleasantness, or wickedness.

O please answer 'who causes the pleasure and pain, who induces love and bondage, who wields final say'?

ते ध्यानयोगानुगता अपश्यन् देवात्मशक्तिं स्वगुणैर्निगूढाम् ।
यः कारणानि निखिलानि तानि कालात्मयुक्तान्यधितिष्ठत्येकः ॥ ३
तमेकनेमिं त्रिवृतं षोडशान्तं शतार्धारं विंशतिप्रत्यराभिः ।
अष्टकैः षड्भिर्विश्वरूपैकपाशं त्रिमार्गभेदं द्विनिमित्तैकमोहम् ॥ ४

te dhyānayogānugatā apaśyan devātmaśaktiṃ svaguṇairnigūḍhām |
yaḥ kāraṇāni nikhilāni tāni kālātmayuktānyadhitiṣṭhatyekaḥ ॥ 3
tamekanemim trivṛtam sodaśāntam śatārdhāram vimśatipratyarābhiḥ
| aṣṭakaiḥ ṣaḍbhirviśvarūpaikapāśaṃ trimārgabhedaṃ
dvinimittaikamoham ॥ 4

ते those seekers ध्यान-योग-अनुगताः inner union inward
travelled अपश्यन् saw देव-आत्म-शक्तिं luminous soul energy स्व-
गुणैः with distinct attributes निगूढाम् । fully cladded. यः who
कारणानि causes निखिलानि all completely तानि those (questions
contemplated) काल-आत्म-युक्तानि Time-Soul-combinations
अधि-तिष्ठति over rules एकः ॥ the One.
तम् him एक-नेमिं single circumference त्रि-वृतं three wheels
षोडश-अन्तं sixteen ends शत-अर्ध-अरं hundred-half spokes
विंशति-प्रत्यराभिः । by twenty counter spokes अष्टकैः sets of eight
षड्भिः with six विश्व-रूप-एक-पाशं gigantic form single belt त्रि-मार्ग-
भेदं three paths distinct द्वि-निमित्तैक-मोहम् ॥ two fold
projection.

1.3 after a long time, through persistent discipline and thorough brain storming, the minds became still. Thought waves stopped. It is then that the clouds of emotions parted, deep-set dusty memories got erased, oscillatory thought beams were lifted, and the source was revealed.

It also became apparent that the dense fog of collective emotions memories thoughts was a perfect barrier that kept the source unnoticed, unsought, un-aimed for, as if non-existent.

This veiled entity was then the Source, the Object of their study, the target of their integrated efforts. It became clear that something that lay hidden beyond the impenetrable mantle of emotionMemoryThought was both the key and the foundation. It was what willed over time and timelessness, it was what gave form to space, names to individuals and infused life and desire in all.

1.4 Those brilliant students then framed mathematical equations for their conclusions. Their hypothesis after extensive cross-checking and collective note comparing gave birth to a physical prototype.

It was agreed that the Source could be considered of as having a crystalline structure consisting of an outer illuminated circle that spanned the entire 360 degree visible spectrum. The first theorem proved was that the Source had complete access in each direction. It knew, sensed, or could foresee each plan, each motive, and everyone's deepest longing. Then the second theorem proved was that the

Source had total control over each outcome, phenomenon, construct whether imaginary or physical.

So a model prototype was drawn on paper and then given shape using steel, wood, glass, clay, paint and ceramic.

This illuminated circle projected triple beams of laser like intensity to reach out and rule over its domain. It was also simultaneously apparent that the Source Control had some stark differences wrt modern control and combat strategies. 1. The Source was equally at ease and retained its fullness and cheerful enthusiasm irrespective of whether its diktat was followed, opposed, or not followed. The controlling beams were tuned to allow equal probability for success, failure, and the impossible.

Each energy beam could be further differentiated into sixteen composite waves. Sixteen is technically the accepted year for love making or explosive virility. Sixteen is technically the age of manhood or womanliness. Most humans reach body proportion, comeliness, and decision making maturity, hence in class XI a student gets to choose his stream for University graduation, opposite sex dating, and coronation.

Thus each energy beam had sixteen modules, to account for and allow 1. Hope 2. Fear 3. Passion 4. Sloth 5. Justice 6. Cruelty 7. Merit 8. Hypocrisy 9. Hardness 10. Sublimity 11. To 16. Reserved for each man and animal, each matter particle, each energy and wave to specify their own favorite attribute.

When we say each beam has sixteen concurrent channels, we mean that the energy beam has reached limiting magnitude or has attained terminal velocity, so that its target is easy pie. Its purpose fulfillment is guaranteed.

The Math also lays great stress on the number 20, as our Brahman prototype is thought of as not possible of unveiling unless we do effort of a 20 minute meditation, or a 20 strokes bhastrika, or an education process that moves us to age 20 (class 12+3years of graduation).

Many common animals like dogs, cats, sheep, and cows, all live to a ripe age of twenty. Many sportsmen and world famous personalities give a glimpse of their talent at this age.

6x8 = 48, this number was introduced to specify six milestones in life. Birth Growth Turbulence Repair Success Dissolution. These six parameters mark the journey of each thing and being, whether living or non-living. Each parameter has a specific period and position.

Eight means the 8 fundamental bodies. Viz.
<u>8 fundamental particles.</u> String Quark Meson Electron Proton Neutron Atom Molecule.
<u>8 fundamental tissues.</u> Bone, bone marrow, blood, plasma, lymphatic fluids, muscle, fat, nerves.
<u>8 fundamental nutritions.</u> Protein, vitamin, fibre, fat, carbohydrate, mineral, water, sunlight.
<u>8 fundamental forces.</u> Gravity, light, magnetism, acceleration, electricity, centrifugal, heat, entropy.

(Source was later christened Brahman, triple beams got named Sattva Rajas Tamas.)

Now the theorem proposed and verified pertained to whether Brahman needed many energies and many devices and many processes to oversee and lord over this infinite spectacle. The prototype said only a single fiber emanating from Brahman attended to each and every thing and being, situation and emotion, black hole and galaxy. Unlike the sun that fires a million rays, only one ray from Brahman processed, inspired, subjugated or elevated each and every known and unknown particle and energy, man, beast, gadget, storm, lightening, fusion, fission, waywardness, responsibility, or love.

As if by magic the prototype made a mirror image, depicting the twosome - boys and girls, cold and hot, rage and romance, black and white. Using imperceptible design, Brahman gave a reasoning mind and an emotional heart, those who failed to balance the two were termed normal status quo who would dissolve after 400 years, those who achieved equilibrium achieved unity and lived the remaining years as a jivan mukta, enlightened and free, content and complete.

(Also refer Chandogya Upanishad verse 3.12.6, 6.1.4, 8.2.1).

To further validate this prototype, a test group of 100 scientists was divided into two, one set looked at one prototype from various angles and went into deep contemplation, the other group studied the other prototype and ran various experiments. In the end the data of both groups of 50 scientists was tabled, and a perfect match was found, thus was accepted by all the supremacy of Brahman, and the theorems went into print as fundamental ideas.

पञ्चस्रोतोम्बुं पञ्चयोन्युग्रवक्रां पञ्चप्राणोर्मि पञ्चबुद्ध्यादिमूलाम् ।
पञ्चावर्तां पञ्चदुःखौघवेगां पञ्चाशद्भेदां पञ्चपर्वामधीमः ॥ ५

pañcasrotombuṃ pañcayonyugravakrāṃ pañcaprāṇormiṃ
pañcabuddhyādimūlām | pañcāvartāṃ pañcaduḥkhaughavegāṃ
pañcāśadbhedāṃ pañcaparvamadhīmaḥ ‖ 5

पञ्च-स्रोतोऽम्बुं five streams water पञ्च-योनि-उग्र-वक्रां five forms
fierce shaped पञ्च-प्राणोर्मि five circulatory forces पञ्च-बुद्धि-आदि-
मूलाम् । of fivefold perception the primal source. पञ्च-आवर्तां
five frequencies पञ्च-दुःख-ओघवेगां of five dangerous rapids
पञ्चाशत्-भेदां of fifty discriminations पञ्च-पर्वाम् of five sectioned
अधीमः ॥ we contemplate on him.

1.5 For other sincere seekers, or later to come scientists and saints, a five-fold methodology was made the benchmark. Pancakosha meditation formed the basis as taught by Sri Sri Ravi Shankar in the Happiness program. By this meditation, a man could hope to grasp the essence and embark on the path of Truth.

Even young children could be taught to identify the five basic senses and their importance, and be inspired to take good care of their eyes and teeth and ears and tongue.

Even people who worked very hard and had difficulty in balancing time or making both ends meet could be induced to go for panchakarma sessions for peak performance at work and play.

Scientists and Pioneers could be taught in detail the laws pertaining to the five great elements, so that they could come up with pragmatic inventions and fantastic discoveries.

Spiritual seekers could learn about the five modulations of the thoughts - proof, sleep, memory, inference, fertile imagination and thus stay on the path.

Businessmen, Administrators and defense forces could learn how to use the 5 weaknesses - anger, lust, vanity, infatuation, righteousness to their advantage.

Doctors and Medics would benefit immensely by understanding the five major systems - respiration, circulation, digestion, evacuation.

For Society, Nation and Civilization to flourish the 50 activities, departments, portfolios were made mandatory.

1 Farming 2 Education 3 Health 4 Defense 5 industry 6 research 7 atmosphere 8 ocean 9 mining 10 recycling 11 retail 12 housing 13 roads 14 parks 15 forests 16 wildlife sanctuary 17 food processing 18 cultural festivities 19 tourism 20 spiritual training awakening 21 exercise 22 sports 23 sanitation 24 pregnant mother and newborn 25 religious 26 electricity generation distribution 27 water generation distribution 28 telecom 29 transportation of cargo livestock 30 travel 31 cooking gas generation distribution 32 archaeology 33 planetary inhabitation 34 deep space study 35 galactic travel 36 weather forecast 37 insurance 38 law and order 39 indoor games 40 romance and honeymoon 41 marriage rituals 42 separation guidelines 43 birth and death registry 44 passport and visa 45 entertainment 46 war 47 hospitality 48 nursing 49 baby sitting 50 post death formalities.

सर्वाजीवे सर्वसंस्थे बृहन्ते अस्मिन् हंसो भ्राम्यते ब्रह्मचक्रे ।
पृथगात्मानं प्रेरितारं च मत्वा जुष्टस्ततस्तेनामृतत्वमेति ॥ ६

sarvājīve sarvasaṃsthe bṛhante asmin haṃso bhrāmyate
brahmacakre | pṛthagātmānaṃ preritāraṃ ca matvā
juṣṭastatastenāmṛtatvameti ॥ 6

सर्वा-जीवे in which all beings live सर्व-संस्थे in which all rest बृहन्ते in the infinite अस्मिन् in this हंसः transmigratory soul भ्राम्यते wanders ब्रह्म-चक्रे । in the cosmic web. पृथक् the individual आत्मानं soul प्रेरितारं is the inspiring life force च and मत्वा having understood जुष्टः pleased ततः thereafter तेन by Him अमृतत्वम् ultimate nectar एति ॥ obtains.

1.6 the car and its driver, the mobile phone and its user, the lathe machine and its operator, all aspire to behold Brahman. Sometimes Brahman satisfies the inventor, at other times he blesses the user, and then there are moments when his grace elevates the instrument - the automobile the spoon the tennis ball or the dawg.

Rare is the son who glimpses the divine in his father, many are fathers who sense the Brahman in their offspring. A few cities get a mayor or dc worth his salt, few anyways can't stand him and wish such a noble soul's early exit.

Who is Brahman wonder the sages, in whom is Brahman's current strongest? The theory that he is omnipresent is possibly misapplied, for the sages say Brahman can be omnipresent at will, not that he is there all the time. Likewise Brahman can be omnipotent by choice, not that decides to win every game, or subdue each opponent.

In the end it is agreed by minute study of a large number of events over a large timeSpace continuum that Brahman alone picks the winner, albeit it is found in the majority of cases he picks someone who is sincere dedicated enduring humble and patient.

उद्गीतमेतत्परमं तु ब्रह्म तस्मिंस्त्रयं सुप्रतिष्ठाऽक्षरं च ।
अत्रान्तरं ब्रह्मविदो विदित्वा लीना ब्रह्मणि तत्परा योनिमुक्ताः ॥ ७

udgītametatparamaṃ tu brahma tasmiṃstrayaṃ supratiṣṭhā'kṣaraṃ ca | atrāntaraṃ brahmavido viditvā līnā brahmaṇi tatparā yonimuktāḥ ॥ 7

उद्गीतम् एतत् this परमं Supreme तु moreover ब्रह्म Brahman तस्मिन् in that त्रयं triad सु-प्रतिष्ठा firm foundation अक्षरं undecaying च । also. अत्र here अन्तरं the essence ब्रह्म-विदः the knowers of Brahman विदित्वा having understood लीनाः merge ब्रह्मणि into Brahman तत्पराः sincerely devoted योनि-मुक्ताः ॥ form & inclination freed.

1.7 On further investigation it is established that Brahman is not at all one-sided, nor does he harbor ill-will, bitterness, frustration or anxiety.

In each being Brahman chooses to play a role, whether the sensuous mind, or the longing heart, or the talented intellect. Sometimes he plays more than one role in a being, in other beings he plays no role at all.

Likewise Brahman may also choose to be the batsman, the bowler or the fielder. He may choose to be a) the pudding b) the act of eating and c) the hungry being. All three at once, one or more of these three, or none at all.

However for sure Brahman is the playground, he is the life, he is the cheering, he is the trophy. Assimilating this fact with a resounding solidarity, the sages got grounded in faith.

This faith became their armor. This faith cleared away all obstacles, this faith made them blissful and divine.

(Also refer Kena Upanishad verse 1.3, 1.4 Brihadaranyaka 3.8.8).

संयुक्तमेतत् क्षरमक्षरं च व्यक्ताव्यक्तं भरते विश्वमीशः ।

अनीशश्चात्मा बध्यते भोक्तृभावाज्ज्ञात्वा देवं मुच्यते सर्वपाशैः ॥ ८

ज्ञाज्ञौ द्वावजावीशानीशावजा ह्येका भोक्तृभोग्यार्थयुक्ता ।

अनन्तश्चात्मा विश्वरूपो ह्यकर्ता त्रयं यदा विन्दते ब्रह्ममेतत् ॥ ९

saṃyuktametat kṣaramakṣaram ca vyaktāvyaktam bharate viśvamīśaḥ | anīśaścātmā badhyate bhoktṛbhāvājjñātvā devaṃ mucyate sarvapāśaiḥ || 8

jñājñau dvāvajāvīśanīśāvajā hyekā bhoktṛbhogyārthayuktā | anantaścātmā viśvarūpo hyakartā trayaṃ yadā vindate brahmametat || 9

संयुक्तम् beautiful combination एतत् this क्षरम् perishable अक्षरं imperishable च and व्यक्त-अव्यक्तं manifest unmanifest भरते supports विश्वम् universe ईशः । the Lord. अनीशः the dependent च and आत्मा Soul बध्यते gets attached भोक्तृ-भावात् sensuous pleasures ज्ञात्वा having known देवं the Divine मुच्यते is freed सर्व-पाशैः ॥ from all bonds.

ज्ञ-अज्ञौ conscious and unconscious द्वौ both अजौ unborn ईश-नीशौ Lord and Devotee (vedic usage) अजा unborn हि Oh! एका she भोक्तृ-भोगि-अर्थ-युक्ता । worldy enjoyments and its enjoyer relationship अनन्तः infinite च and आत्मा Self विश्व-रूपः universal हि Oh! अ-कर्ता non-doer त्रयं threesome यदा when विन्दते realizes ब्रह्मम् Brahman (vedic usage) एतत् ॥ this.

1.8 - 9 A further corollary was added to the thesis. To lay at rest all discrimination and differentiation, it was stated - Brahman himself chose to manifest in differing degrees of radiance.

He manifested along the entire spectrum 0 to 1 and all in between. He manifested in all names and forms from $-\infty$ to $+\infty$. He made himself superbly intelligent or abysmally dull. Most beautiful or thoroughly unwanted.

Still He ensured that each name and form had some likes at some point in the spaceTime continuum, none went altogether without food, love or friendship.

क्षरं प्रधानममृताक्षरं हरः क्षरात्मानावीशाते देव एकः ।

तस्याभिध्यानाद्योजनात्तत्त्वभावात् भूयश्चान्ते विश्वमायानिवृत्तिः ॥ १०

ज्ञात्वा देवं सर्वपाशापहानिः क्षीणैः क्लैशैर्जन्ममृत्युप्रहाणिः ।

तस्याभिध्यानात्तृतीयं देहभेदे विश्वैश्वर्यं केवल आप्तकामः ॥ ११

ksaram pradhānamamrtāksaram harah ksarātmānāvīśate deva ekah
| tasyābhidhyānādyojanāttattvabhāvāt bhūyaścānte

viśvamāyānivṛttih ॥ 10

jñātvā devam sarvapāśāpahānih ksīnaih klaiśairjanmamrtyuprahānih
| tasyābhidhyānāttṛtīyam dehabhede viśvaiśvaryam kevala

āptakāmah ॥ 11

क्षरं perishable प्रधानम् matter अमृत-अक्षरं immortal undecaying हरः Lord Shiva क्षर-आत्मानौ body and jiva ईशते lords over देवः the Lord एकः । the One. तस्य of his अभि-ध्यानात् by deep contemplation योजनात् by feeling oneness तत्त्व-भावात् by essential connection भूयः becoming च and अन्ते in the end विश्व-माया-निवृत्तिः ॥ world projection cessation.

ज्ञात्वा having perceived देवं the Divine सर्व-पाश-अपहानिः all bindings vanish क्षीणैः with diminishing क्लैशैः of distresses जन्म-मृत्यु-प्रहाणिः । cycle of ups and downs disappears. तस्य on Him अभि-ध्यानात् by profound meditation तृतीयं third state (neither up nor down) देह-भेदे body consciousness discriminates विश्व-ऐश्वर्यं world emperorship केवलः singular आप्त-कामः ॥ fulfilled all desire.

1.10 - 11 Body is said to be composed of 5 elements that have been blessed to occupy a finite cloud in the timeSpace continuum.

Within this timeSpace cloud, this body is permanent, long lasting and imperishable. Once in specific albeit uncharted moments, Brahman touches this cloud. In other words the Shiva consciousness called "Hara" pulsates and its vibration unites with the timeSpace cloud, though it cannot be established how or when.

The sages can only establish and validate that having distinctly heard these words from the Master, one must become one-pointed in contemplation, again and again seeking to reinforce the Brahman presence. For sure then as if some gates open, as if some dimensions get unlocked, one gets transported to the Brahman plane, merging, uniting, becoming one.

This merging or dissolution or nirvana or enlightenment cannot be sensed by oneself nor by any other self.

There is no outer or visible change, the game continues as before, however instincts like fear, hate, guilt, bitterness, stubbornness bid final adieu.

एतज्ज्ञेयं नित्यमेवात्मसंस्थं नातः परं वेदितव्यं हि किञ्चित् । भोक्ता भोग्यं
प्रेरितारं च मत्वा सर्वं प्रोक्तं त्रिविधं ब्रह्ममेतत् ॥ १२ वह्नेर्यथा योनिगतस्य मूर्तिर्न
दृश्यते नैव च लिङ्गनाशः । स भूय एवेन्धनयोनिगृह्यस्तद्वोभयं वै प्रणवेन देहे ॥
१३ स्वदेहमरणिं कृत्वा प्रणवं चोत्तरारणिम् । ध्याननिर्मथनाभ्यासाद्देवं
पश्यन्निगूढवत् ॥ १४ etajjñeyaṃ nityamevātmasaṃsthaṃ nātaḥ paraṃ
veditavyaṃ hi kiñcit | bhoktā bhogyaṃ preritāraṃ ca matvā
sarvaṃ proktaṃ trividhaṃ brahmametat ॥ 12 vahneryathā
yonigatasya mūrtirna dṛśyate naiva ca liṅganāśaḥ | sa bhūya
evendhanayonigṛhyastadvobhayaṃ vai praṇavena dehe ॥ 13
svadehamaraṇiṃ kṛtvā praṇavaṃ cottarāraṇim |
dhyānanirmathanābhyāsāddevaṃ paśyannigūḍhavat ॥ 14
एतत् this ज्ञेयं be known नित्यम् never ending एव alone आत्म-संस्थं
in Self properly established न not अतः beyond परं the
Supreme वेदितव्यं to be realized हि Oh! किञ्चित् । anything.
भोक्ता the enjoyer भोग्यं the enjoyed प्रेरितारं ultimate enjoyment
giver च and मत्वा having contemplated सर्वं all प्रोक्तं have
proclaimed त्रि-विधं three aspects ब्रह्म(म्) of Brahman एतत् ॥
this. वह्नेः luminosity यथा as योनि-गतस्य form having
transcended मूर्तिः solid form न not दृश्यते visible नैव not only च
and लिङ्ग-नाशः । guise uncovered. सः he भूयः becoming एव
alone इन्धन-योनि-गृह्यः fuel from form is obtained तत् that वा or
उभयं before and after वै indeed प्रणवेन by OM chanting देहे ॥ in
the body. स्व-देहम् own body अरणि lower part of anatomy कृत्वा
having done प्रणवं OM च and उत्तर-अरणिम् । upper part of
anatomy. ध्यान-निर्मथन-अभ्यासात् by practice of deep
contemplatation देवं the divine light पश्यन् perceiving निगूढवत्
॥ as deep inside.

1.12 by astute discrimination and differentiation One's mind can be separated into three - my desires, desires of my loved one(s), desirelessness.

The student must strive strongly to arrive at this demarcation. Taking copious notes can be of assistance, listening to the words of the Master can be helpful, being in the company of the wise is also fruitful.

1.13 - 14 Another potent technique to arrive in the Brahman space is the sacred syllable Om.

Just as striking a matchstick causes spontaneous birth of fire. But who applies this fact? Only the one who has been so taught and has the proper matchstick. The uninitiated will find it practically impossible to create fire from two pieces of wood.

Analogy of light hidden in wood to suggest Brahman can manifest in any body.

Similarly Om gets infused with radiance only when learnt from the Master, then its assiduous practice brings us so close to Brahman that it reveals itself.

The practice is Sanatan, it can be done variously by various folk. The teaching is also Sanatan, Masters across the continents may teach in any number of ways.

What is common is the commitment, the earnestness, the continuity, and utter lack of righteousness (I right thee wrong).

तिलेषु तैलं दधनीव सर्पिरापः स्रोतःस्वरणीषु चाग्निः ।
एवमात्मात्मनि गृह्यतेऽसौ सत्येनैनं तपसा योऽनुपश्यति ॥१५
सर्वव्यापिनमात्मानं क्षीरे सर्पिरिवार्पितम् ।
आत्मविद्यातपोमूलं तद्ब्रह्मोपनिषत् परम् । तद्ब्रह्मोपनिषत् परम् ॥ १६

tileṣu tailaṃ dadhanīva sarpirāpaḥ srotaḥsvaraṇīṣu cāgniḥ |
evamātmātmani gṛhyate'sau satyenainaṃ tapasā yo'nupaśyati ॥15
sarvavyāpinamātmānaṃ kṣīre sarpirivārpitam |
ātmavidyātapomūlaṃ tadbrahmopaniṣat param |
tadbrahmopaniṣat param ॥ 16

तिलेषु in sesame seeds तैलं oil दधनि in curd इव as सर्पिः butter आपः water स्रोतःसु in springs अरणीषु in wood च and अग्निः । fire. एवम् verily आत्मा Self आत्मनि in Soul गृह्यते is observed असौ this सत्येन by truthfulness एनं that तपसा by austerity यः who अनुपश्यति ॥ recognizes. सर्व-व्यापिनम् omnipresent आत्मानं Self क्षीरे in milk सर्पिः butter इव like अर्पितम् । contained (is). आत्म-विद्या-तपो-मूलं having source in purified Self knowledge तद् that ब्रह्म Brahman उपनिषत् resolves doubts परम् । Ultimate. तद् that ब्रह्म Brahman उपनिषत् dissolves grief परम् ॥ Supreme.

1.15 - 16 Oil or fluid is a natural ingredient in seeds, but its extraction needs vision, method, planning, hard work and time. Only a few entrepreneurs make the top grade in this regard.

The calves and young of mammals drink only milk, but man processes the same to produce a plethora of tasty byproducts. Not everyone has the skill to make delicious cottage cheese, or yummy yoghurt, or a mouthwatering rasgulla.

Water of springs and glaciers is highly recommended, however that access is limited to a paltry segment of the population.

Similarly to learn the deepest secrets of the mind, to learn to discriminate and separate layer by layer the bundle of memory and emotion, is not everyone's cup of tea.

Seek out a master who can guide, then serve him and satisfy him to the fullest, it's possible then for Brahman to fall into your lap.

This is the gist of the wisdom that dawned on those brave adventurers who sought out the Truth with exemplary efforts.

2nd Teaching (yogic techniques)

(This chapter lists some practical methods for progressing on the path of yoga).

Surya Namaskar

द्वितीयोऽध्यायः

युञ्जानः प्रथमं मनस्तत्त्वाय सविता धियः ।

अग्नेर्ज्योतिर्निचाय्य पृथिव्या अध्याभरत् ॥ १

युक्तेन मनसा वयं देवस्य सवितुः सवे । सुवर्गेयाय शक्त्या ॥ २

युक्त्वाय मनसा देवान् सुवर्यतो धिया दिवम् ।

बृहज्ज्योतिः करिष्यतः सविता प्रसुवाति तान् ॥ ३

dvitīyo'dhyāyaḥ

yuñjānaḥ prathamaṃ manastattvāya savitā dhiyaḥ |

agnerjyotirnicāyya pṛthivyā adhyābharat || 1 || yuktena manasā

vayaṃ devasya savituḥ save | suvargeyāya śaktyā || 2 ||

yuktvāya manasā devān suvaryato dhiyā divam | bṛhajjyotiḥ

kariṣyataḥ savitā prasuvāti tān || 3

युञ्जानः integrating प्रथमं first मनः the mind तत्त्वाय for attaining the essence सविता effulgent sun within धियः । the intellect. अग्नेः of the flame ज्योतिः the light निचाय्य having discriminated पृथिव्याः out of the soil अध्याभरत् ॥ distilled. युक्तेन by integration मनसा by mind and senses वयं we देवस्य of the self-luminous सवितुः of inner glow सवे । to express. सुवर्गेयाय for highest bliss शक्त्या ॥ with sincere effort. युक्त्वाय for uniting मनसा by the mind देवान् luminosities सुवर्यतः supreme धिया by logical reasoning दिवम् । heavenly. बृहत् magnificent ज्योतिः light करिष्यतः shall endeavor सविता sun within प्रसुवाति give joyous expression तान् ॥ them.

2.1

To begin with, the aspirant should start with Surya Namaskar, a set of 12 asanas. That quickly strengthens the digestive system, so the senses begin to shed their waywardness.

2.2 the practice can be enhanced with chanting and meditation, and an optimal beginning should include 12 or 24 rounds of Surya Namaskar.

2.3 additionally we can face the eastern direction if possible. In the morning the sunlight is beneficial for the eyes and skin.

युञ्जते मन उत युञ्जते धियो विप्रा विप्रस्य बृहतो विपश्चितः ।
वि होत्रा दधे वयुनाविदेक इन्मही देवस्य सवितुः परिष्टुतिः ॥ ४
युजे वां ब्रह्म पूर्व्यं नमोभिर्विश्लोक एतु पथ्येव सूरेः ।
श्रृण्वन्तु विश्वे अमृतस्य पुत्रा आ ये धामानि दिव्यानि तस्थुः ॥ ५
अग्नियत्राभिमथ्यते वायुर्यत्राधिरुध्यते ।
सोमो यत्रातिरिच्यते तत्र सञ्जायते मनः ॥ ६

yuñjate mana uta yuñjate dhiyo viprā viprasya bṛhato vipaścitaḥ ।
vi hotrā dadhe vayunāvideka inmahī devasya savituḥ pariṣṭutiḥ ॥
4 ॥ yuje vāṃ brahma pūrvyaṃ namobhirviśloka etu pathyeva sūreḥ
। śṛṇvantu viśve amṛtasya putrā ā ye dhāmāni divyāni tasthuḥ ॥ 5
॥ agniryatrābhimathyate vāyuryatrādhirudhyate । somo
yatrātiricyate tatra sañjāyate manaḥ ॥ 6

युञ्जते balancing मनः the mind उत or else युञ्जते integrating धियः self-restraint विप्राः the wise विप्रस्य of the intelligent बृहतः great विपश्चितः । Brahman. वि होत्राः spiritual disciplines दधे (विदधे) specially undergoes वयुनाविद् scholar एकः one इत् alone मही wonderful देवस्य of self-luminosity सवितुः of inner divinity परिष्टुतिः ॥ glorification. युजे i merge वां thee two ब्रह्म Brahman पूर्व्यं ancient नमोभिः by meditation विश्लोकः the mighty standard एतु may manifest पथि in keeping the goal एव alone सूरेः । of the wise. श्रृण्वन्तु may listen विश्वे अमृतस्य of blissful पुत्राः sons आ ये who धामानि areas दिव्यानि heavenly तस्थुः (आतस्थुः) ॥ should get stationed. अग्निः fire यत्र where अभिमथ्यते comes alive by churning वायुः air यत्र where अधिरुध्यते । starts blowing by fanning सोमः juice of pleasure यत्र where अतिरिच्यते overflows तत्र there सञ्जायते attains beatitude मनः ॥ the mind and reasoning faculty.

2.4 over time one must learn to chant the mantras for each posture, since sound is a powerful modulator of the mind.

2.5 treating the sun as a friend and being grateful for his presence in life is another means of making good progress on the path of yoga. Talk to the sun, allow its rays to touch the entire body for 20 minutes. Especially eyes, nabhi, spine, hands, feet.

2.6 the morning fire ritual known as agnihotra in which two offerings of ghee are made to a small fire along with invoking the sun deity is also a technique to stabilize oneself on the path of yoga. This ritual needs no initiation, young children can do and feel their eyesight become brighter, the elderly can feel their joints are getting stronger.

सवित्रा प्रसवेन जुषेत ब्रह्म पूर्व्यम् । तत्र योनिं कृणवसे न हि ते पूर्तमक्षिपत् ॥ ७

त्रिरुन्नतं स्थाप्य समं शरीरं हृदीन्द्रियाणि मनसा सन्निवेश्य ।

ब्रह्मोडुपेन प्रतरेत विद्वान् स्रोतांसि सर्वाणि भयावहानि ॥ ८

प्राणान् प्रपीड्येह संयुक्तचेष्टः क्षीणे प्राणे नासिकयोच्छ्वसीत ।

दुष्टाश्वयुक्तमिव वाहमेनं विद्वान् मनो धारयेताप्रमत्तः ॥ ९

savitrā prasavena juṣeta brahma pūrvyam | tatra yoniṃ kṛṇavase na hi te pūrtamakṣipat || 7 || trirunnataṃ sthāpya samaṃ śarīraṃ hṛdīndriyāṇi manasā sanniveśya | brahmoḍupena pratareta vidvān srotāṃsi sarvāṇi bhayāvahāni || 8 || prāṇān prapīḍyeha saṃyuktaceṣṭaḥ kṣīṇe prāṇe nāsikayocchvasīta | duṣṭāśvayuktamiva vāhamenaṃ vidvān mano dhārayetāpramattaḥ || 9

सवित्रा with Brahman प्रसवेन with Source जुषेत should engage in ब्रह्म Brahman पूर्व्यम् । primal. तत्र there योनिं the form कृणवसे throwing off न do not हि verily ते they पूर्तम् prior actions अक्षिपत् ॥ hurting. त्रि-रुन्नतं triad of head-neck- torso स्थाप्य holding समं nice and straight शरीरं the anatomy हृदि in the heart इन्द्रियाणि all senses मनसा by reason सन्निवेश्य । properly place and enter. ब्रह्म-उडुपेन with Brahman's raft प्रतरेत must efficiently cross over विद्वान् the intelligent one स्रोतांसि rapids सर्वाणि all भयावहानि ॥ dangerous. प्राणान् life forces and goals प्रपीड्य by determined effort इह here and now संयुक्तचेष्टः क्षीणे प्राणे नासिकया उच्छ्वसीत । दुष्ट-अश्व-युक्तम् uncontrollable horse reigning in इव like वाहम् the reins एनं this विद्वान् the noble one मनः the mind धारयेत् must bravely reign in अप्रमत्तः ॥ without distraction.

2.7 whatever it is, have a place for the sun in your heart. Any which way you can, make the sun worthy of your attention. This technique is also proven to be an asset on the path of yoga.

E.g. sun meditation as guided by Sri Sri Ravi Shankar. Sun exercises as taught in the Netra Jyoti panchakarma.

2.8 a favorite method involves Keeping the Spine Straight, Torso absolutely still like a statue. Now take your Sahaj Mantra with faint attention in the heart chakra at the center of the chest. Do it cheerfully, without restlessness. If needed play a vigorous game and allow muscles to become warmed, mind to become focused, before attempting this.

2.9 another process involves rhythmic breath as taught by Sri Sri Ravi Shankar in the famed Happiness Course. All the breathing here is through the nose. At the end of the Sudarshan Kriya, ensure that one goes into a relaxed posture for a few minutes, shavasana preferably, so that the Mind can disengage from the senses, the intellect and memory can disconnect from the self, and utter peace is given a chance to correct all imbalances. The shavasana is very much needed to infuse each cell with the nectar generated, don't skip the lying down detox part.

समे शुचौ शर्करावह्निवालुका विवर्जिते शब्दजलाश्रयादिभिः ।
मनोनुकूले न तु चक्षुपीडने गुहानिवाताश्रयणे प्रयोजयेत् ॥ १०
नीहारधूमार्कानिलानलानां खद्योतविद्युत्स्फटिकशशीनाम् ।
एतानि रूपाणि पुरःसराणि ब्रह्मण्यभिव्यक्तिकराणि योगे ॥ ११
पृथ्व्यप्तेजोऽनिलखे समुत्थिते पञ्चात्मके योगगुणे प्रवृत्ते ।
न तस्य रोगो न जरा न मृत्युः प्राप्तस्य योगाग्निमयं शरीरम् ॥ १२

same śucau śarkarāvahnivālukā vivarjite śabdajalāśrayādibhiḥ ǀ manonukūle na tu cakṣupīḍane guhānivātāśrayaṇe prayojayet ǁ 10 ǁ nīhāradhūmārkānilānalānāṃ khadyotavidyutsphaṭikaśaśīnām ǀ etāni rūpāṇi puraḥsarāṇi brahmaṇyabhivyaktikarāṇi yoge ǁ 11 ǁ pṛthvyaptejo'nilakhe samutthite pañcātmake yogaguṇe pravṛtte ǀ na tasya rogo na jarā na mṛtyuḥ prāptasya yogāgnimayaṃ śarīram ǁ 12 ǁ समे in an even शुचौ in a clean शर्करा-वह्नि-वालुका pebbles-open fires-dust विवर्जिते devoid of शब्द-जलआ-श्रय-आदिभिः ǀ and also of noise-dampness-emotion. मनःअ-नुकूले in helping the mind to focus न not तु and चक्षु-पीडने an eye-sore गुहा-निवातआ-श्रयणे places protected from high winds प्रयोजयेत् ǁ do yogic disciplines. नीहार-धूमअ-कंअ-निलअ-नलानां of mist-smoke- sunlight-breeze-flame खद्योत-विद्युत्स्फ-टिक-शशीनाम् ǀ of firefly-lightning-crystal-moonlike एतानि these रूपाणि forms पुरःसराणि preceding feedbacks ब्रह्मणि of Brahman अभिव्यक्ति-कराणि heralding योगे ǁ during Yogic practices. पृथ्वी-आप्-तेजः-अनिल-खे in earth water fire air space समुउ-त्थिते nicely arising पञ्च-आत्मके fivefold elements योग-गुणे in the Yogic temperament प्रवृत्ते ǀ manifested. न none तस्य his रोगः illness न none जरा weakness न no मृत्युः defeat प्राप्तस्य of getting योग-अग्नि-मयं to yogic fire purified शरीरम् ǁ body mind.

2.10 at a basic level a yoga studio must have even lighting that does not impinge on the eyes, fresh air circulation so enough oxygen levels are maintained, temperate climate control so mind isn't doing unnecessary gymnastics, and clean level flooring of virgin marble or wood.

Gadgets, TV, telephone and other electronic sounds must be avoided so that the inner Om can be heard. Chatter and noises of people talking must be kept to a bare minimum.

It is not recommended to open a yoga studio in a super market or place adjacent to high traffic movement or where babies yell and children squeal.

2.11 During deep meditation, various visions might appear, pay no heed. Do not latch on. Neither block them out, nor engage with them. Do not try to recreate the experience of a session another time.

Each meditation could be different or similar, could have same or disparate effect, just live the experience and move on. Meditation connects to Brahman space, from where one gets to heal one's ancestors as well as descendants, it is hence possible in certain meditative sessions that one feels nothing, since the benefit went to someone else.

2.12 meditations on the 5 elements and the 7 chakras are hugely beneficial. Such meditations give lasting relief from illness, poor health, mental blocks, and cause a remarkable change in temperament and attitude. 5 elements define our barriers, and transcending each gives immense relief. 7 chakras define our milestones and achieving these frees our next birth's burden to that extent.

लघुत्वमारोग्यमलोलुपत्वं वर्णप्रसादं स्वरसौष्ठवं च ।

गन्धः शुभो मूत्रपुरीषमल्पं योगप्रवृत्तिं प्रथमां वदन्ति ॥ १३

यथैव बिम्बं मृदयोपलिप्तं तेजोमयं भ्राजते तत् सुधान्तम् ।

तद्वाऽऽत्मतत्त्वं प्रसमीक्ष्य देही एकः कृतार्थो भवते वीतशोकः ॥ १४

यदात्मतत्त्वेन तु ब्रह्मतत्त्वं दीपोपमेनेह युक्तः प्रपश्येत् ।

अजं ध्रुवं सर्वतत्त्वैर्विशुद्धं ज्ञात्वा देवं मुच्यते सर्वपाशैः ॥ १५

laghutvamārogyamalolupatvaṃ varṇaprasādaṃ svarasauṣṭhavaṃ ca | gandhaḥ śubho mūtrapurīṣamalpaṃ yogapravṛttiṃ prathamāṃ vadanti || 13 || yathaiva bimbaṃ mṛdayopaliptaṃ tejomayaṃ bhrājate tat sudhāntam | tadvā"tmatattvaṃ prasamīkṣya dehī ekaḥ kṛtārtho bhavate vītaśokaḥ || 14 || yadātmatattvena tu brahmatattvaṃ dīpopameneha yuktaḥ prapaśyet | ajaṃ dhruvaṃ sarvatattvairviśuddhaṃ jñātvā devaṃ mucyate sarvapāśaiḥ || 15 ||

लघुत्वम् lightness आरोग्यम् firmness अलोलुपत्वं desirelessness वर्ण-प्रसादं complexion-pleasant स्वर-सौष्ठवं speech-noble च । and. गन्धः odor शुभः agreeable मूत्र-पुरीषम् urine potty अल्पं negligible योग-प्रवृत्ति Yogic quality indications प्रथमां of the first वदन्ति ॥ they say. यथा as एव just बिम्बं reflection मृदया by dirt उपलिप्तं covered तेजोमयं brightly भ्राजते shines तत् it सुधान्तम् । when scrubbed. तद्वा similarly आत्म-तत्त्वं divine soul प्रसम्-ईक्ष्य having perceived देही the jiva एकः one कृतार्थः life's aim भवते achieves वीत-शोकः ॥ free of sorrow. यदा when आत्म-तत्त्वेन by divine light तु moreover ब्रह्म-तत्त्वं Brahman essence दीप-उपमेन by glow resemblance इह here and now युक्तः the Yogi प्रपश्येत् । clearly perceives. अजं unborn ध्रुवं eternal सर्व-तत्त्वैः from all impressions विशुद्धं fully freed ज्ञात्वा realizing देवं the Divine मुच्यते releases सर्व-पाशैः ॥ all bonds.

2.13 and how may we know that we are on correct path? There shall be many indications and feedbacks. Among them

- one feels more energetic and enthusiastic, ready for small tasks or gestures which one earlier shirked from.
- common cold, headache, stomach ache frequency drops.
- reduction in lustful tendency
- remarks of Youthfulness from friends or colleagues
- speech becomes softer, harshness and cruelty of tongue is less
- body odor becomes imperceptible, sweat no longer bothers
- appetite becomes disciplined, one rarely misses food timing or craves for exotic dishes.

2.14 Glimpses of Brahman become more common, frequently one senses the Lord's presence, heart tastes drops of nectar.

Mind feels clear and less cloudy, there is a dip in fear, frustration, anxiety.

A sense of goodwill prevails.

2.15 The call of the soul is heard. The destiny and design come in focus. Distractions and infatuations disappear.

One's efforts become aligned with the Divine will. Joyousness resurfaces.

एष ह देवः प्रदिशोऽनु सर्वाः पूर्वो ह जातः स उ गर्भे अन्तः ।
स एव जातः स जनिष्यमाणः प्रत्यङ् जनास्तिष्ठति सर्वतोमुखः ॥ १६
यो देवो अग्नौ यो अप्सु यो विश्वं भुवनमाविवेश ।
य ओषधीषु यो वनस्पतिषु तस्मै देवाय नमो नमः ॥ १७

eṣa ha devaḥ pradiśo'nu sarvāḥ pūrvo ha jātaḥ sa u garbhe antaḥ ǀ
sa eva jātaḥ sa janiṣyamāṇaḥ pratyaṅ janāstiṣṭhati sarvatomukhaḥ
ǁ 16
yo devo agnau yo apsu yo viśvaṃ bhuvanamāviveśa ǀ ya oṣadhīṣu
yo vanaspatiṣu tasmai devāya namo namaḥ ǁ 17

एषः this ह Oh! देवः the Divine प्र-दिशः various directions अनु within सर्वाः all पूर्वः primal ह verily जातः begot life सः He उ indeed गर्भे in the womb अन्तः ǀ the deep end. सः He एव alone जातः was born सः He जनिष्यमाणः shall be born प्रत्यङ् within जनाः persons तिष्ठति is available सर्वतः-मुखः ǁ all facing. यः which देवः the Divinity अग्नौ inside fire यः which अप्सु inside water यः which विश्वं world भुवनम् structure आविवेश ǀ pervades. यः which ओषधीषु inside herbs यः which वनस्पतिषु inside plants and trees तस्मै to him देवाय to that Divine नमः hearty salutation नमः ǁ humble offering.

2.16 one forgives oneself and slowly learns to forgive others, as the hidden divinity in all become visible.

The deeper layers of consciousness get noticed, the basic building blocks of each being seem more human, friendly, and acceptability increases.

2.17 One becomes friends with the road and with the berm, the lawn and the garden delight our senses, trees becomes precious and sacrosanct.

More efforts are spent in the maintenance of biodiversity and ecology, the rivers and lakes are made clean and fresh, mountains get honored and hiking trails get trekked.

3rd Teaching (deities of Brahman)

Who causes Sleep and Awaking?
Rudra.

<u>तृतीयोऽध्यायः</u>

य एको जालवानीशत ईशनीभिः सर्वाँल्लोकानीशत ईशनीभिः ।

य एवैक उद्भवे सम्भवे च य एतद्विदुरमृतास्ते भवन्ति ॥ १

एको हि रुद्रो न द्वितीयाय तस्थुर्य इमाँल्लोकानीशत ईशनीभिः ।

प्रत्यङ्‌ जनांस्तिष्ठति सञ्चुकोचान्तकाले संसृज्य विश्वा भुवनानि गोपाः ॥ २

tṛtīyo'dhyāyaḥ

ya eko jālavānīśata īśanībhiḥ sarvāṁllokānīśata īśanībhiḥ | ya
evaika udbhave sambhave ca ya etadviduramṛtāste bhavanti || 1

eko hi rudro na dvitīyāya tasthurya imāṁllokānīśata īśanībhiḥ |
pratyaṅ janāṁstiṣṭhati sañcukocāntakāle saṁsṛjya viśvā bhuvanāni
gopāḥ || 2

यः who एकः the one जालवान् the powerful web ईशते rules ईशनीभिः with command सर्वान् all लोकान् galaxies ईशते oversees ईशनीभिः I authoritatively. यः who एव alone एकः the one उद्भवे at the hour of creation सम्भवे at the hour of dissolution च and यः who एतत् this विदुः understand अमृताः immortal ते they भवन्ति ॥ become. एकः one हि alone रुद्रः the Rudra (the Fluid or Juice in creation) न not any द्वितीयाय for the second तस्थुः यः who इमान् these लोकान् worlds ईशते rules ईशनीभिः I with awareness. प्रत्यङ्‌ within (हे) जनाः O people! तिष्ठति is available सञ्चुकोच withdrew unto Himself अन्त-काले at the last hour संसृज्य having carefully projected विश्वा universal भुवनानि structures गोपाः ॥ the guardians.

3.1 When all men wake up, who wakes them up? When all men sleep who puts them to slumber?
Ponder ponder.

When we see incredible talents blossom in men all over the world, who is responsible for infusing them in the first place?

Is there a Lord of the universe? Is there someone who protects the tender saplings and watches over the babies?

Rare are the folk who wonder and ponder on such inscrutable tracks. Those who so venture on these lonely paths, surely attain the Supreme. They get rid of their frustrations and anxieties, they are elevated to a plane bereft of turmoil.

3.2 There is one fluid that flows in each man. This fluid is the same in each, irrespective of different emotions, currents, and tendencies that are secondary and less important.

The common current in all is not easily perceived, it continues unabated and in full strength, irrespective of circumstances, events, age or any phenomena.

विश्वतश्चक्षुरुत विश्वतोमुखो विश्वतोबाहुरुत विश्वतस्पात् ।
सं बाहुभ्यां धमति संपतत्रैर्द्यावाभूमी जनयन् देव एकः ॥३
यो देवानां प्रभवश्चोद्भवश्च विश्वाधिपो रुद्रो महर्षिः ।
हिरण्यगर्भं जनयामास पूर्वं स नो बुद्‌ध्या शुभया संयुनक्तु ॥ ४

viśvataścakṣuruta viśvatomukho viśvatobāhuruta viśvataspāt |
saṃ bāhubhyāṃ dhamati saṃpatatatrairdyāvābhūmī janayan deva
ekaḥ ॥ 3

yo devānāṃ prabhavaścodbhavaśca viśvādhipo rudro maharṣiḥ |
hiraṇyagarbhaṃ janayāmāsa pūrvaṃ sa no buddhyā śubhayā
saṃyunaktu ॥ 4

विश्वतः-चक्षुः universal eye उत Oh! विश्वतः-मुखः universal face
विश्वतः-बाहुः universal hand उत Oh! विश्वतः-पात् । universal foot.
सं बाहुभ्यां by both hands धमति (सं-धमति) greatly excites संपतत्रैः
by feathering द्यावा-भूमी heaven and earth जनयन् projecting
देवः the Lord एकः ॥ the One. यः Who देवानां of perception प्रभवः
the origin च and उद्भवः the generation च and विश्व-अधि-पः
universal overlord रुद्रः Rudra महर्षिः । great Scientist. हिरण्य-
गर्भं virile semen in womb जनयामास projected पूर्वं ancient सः
He नः us all बुद्‌ध्या with intellect शुभया with good संयुनक्तु ॥
may hopefully bless.

3.3 This fluid Rudra inspires eyes and ears to function, and gives wings to emotions.

Rudra causes notions of heaven and divinity, and also supports the physical planets and galaxies. It remains unaltered in all.

3.4 Rudra is an intelligence that senses all things, all actions, all thoughts, and even unspoken emotions.

Rudra is the force that powers the mighty. It is the prime mover of geniuses.

Rudra creates the golden crucibles that seed every entrepreneur and enterprise.

O blessed force! May our intellect see your core plan and understand one's native design, may we appreciate your working in each body.

या ते रुद्र शिवा तनूरघोराऽपापकाशिनी ।
तया नस्तनुवा शन्तमया गिरिशन्ताभिचाकशीहि ॥ ५
यामिषुं गिरिशन्त हस्ते बिभर्ष्यस्तवे ।
शिवां गिरित्र तां कुरु मा हिꣳसीः पुरुषं जगत् ॥ ६

yā te rudra śivā tanūraghorā'pāpakāśinī | tayā nastanuvā
śantamayā giriśantābhicākaśīhi ॥ 5
yābhiṣuṃ giriśanta haste bibharṣyastave | śivāṃ giritra tāṃ kuru
mā hi(guṃ)sīḥ puruṣaṃ jagat ॥ 6

Famous Verse occurs also in Rudra Puja – Krishna Yajurveda

या what ते thy रुद्र O Rudra the Juice! शिवा auspicious energy
तनूः manifested form अ-घोरा not gross अ-पाप-काशिनी । not
mistakes filled. तया by that नः us all तनुवा by ourself शन्त-मया
calming गिरि-शन्त the body gracing one अभिचाकशीहि ॥ should
infuse us with delight. याम् which इषुं arrow energy beam
गिरिशन्त the one inhabiting the scriptures हस्ते in hand बिभर्षि
thou hold अस्तवे । for releasing. शिवां auspicious गिरि-त्र O
protector of creation तां that कुरु please do मा do not हिंसीः
harm पुरुषं the Lord जगत् ॥ the creation.

3.5 O Rudra, most auspicious one!
O thee that pervades every body, may the cruelty in us be
muted, may our vengeance and rage prove fruitless.

May you enforce calmness in mind and softness in heart.
May you throw proper light on the scriptures so that we do
not learn them incorrectly.

May you drop down to our level of understanding and aid us
in choosing the teaching with simple vocabulary, and thus
prevent our intellect from being clouded.

3.6 O the exciter and the cause of virility! Kindly ensure
that my energy causes no harm, my action and speech are
not misdirected. My aim is true.

ततः परं ब्रह्मपरं बृहन्तं यथानिकायं सर्वभूतेषु गूढम् ।
विश्वस्यैकं परिवेष्टितारमीशं तं ज्ञात्वाऽमृता भवन्ति ॥ ७
tataḥ param brahmaparam bṛhantam yathānikāyam sarvabhūteṣu
gūḍham | viśvasyaikam pariveṣṭitāramīśam tam jñātvā'mṛtā
bhavanti ॥ 7

ततः than परं the highest ब्रह्म-परं the Brahman supreme बृहन्तं
the infinite यथा-निकायं as per bodily form सर्व-भूतेषु in all beings
गूढम् । deeply placed. विश्वस्य of the universe एकं the one
परिवेष्टितारम् the supreme envelop ईशं the Lord तं Him ज्ञात्वा
having understood अमृताः above ups and downs भवन्ति ॥
become.

वेदाहमेतं पुरुषं महान्तमादित्यवर्णं तमसः परस्तात् ।
तमेव विदित्वाऽतिमृत्युमेति नान्यः पन्था विद्यतेऽयनाय ॥ ८
vedāhametam puruṣam mahāntamādityavarṇam tamasaḥ parastāt
| tameva viditvā'timṛtyumeti nānyaḥ panthā vidyate'yanāya ॥ 8

वेद having realized अहम् i एतं this पुरुषं Being महान्तम् great
आदित्य-वर्णं sun-like luminous तमसः ignorance परस्तात् । wholly
beyond. तम् Him एव alone विदित्वा having realized अति-मृत्युम्
beyond the clutches एति evolves न not अन्यः another पन्थाः
path विद्यते is known अयनाय ॥ for evolution.

3.7 That elusive force within each is hard to perceive, yet is the governor of all great acts.

When we do the exceptional, when the incredible results through us, it is this Supreme current that flows in the creation that gets the credit, not any individual person.

The rare traveller who discerns this eternal hand reaches that plane devoid of sorrow. He is transported to the plane of abundance, where there is no lack.

3.8 O lucky me! I seem to have glimpsed the Supreme Soul, the self-luminous, the one whom darkness does not obscure.

Ignorance only veils thee, it cannot overcome thee.

O lucky me! I feel so comforted and at ease, i feel free. I now move unobstructed and my actions are unthwarted. Methinks only someone who can dig deep within and uncover thee can access the universe's key. Only such a bold and persevering man might taste freedom and live full untainted by regret.

यस्मात् परं नापरमस्ति किञ्चिद्यस्मान्नाणीयो न ज्यायोऽस्ति कश्चित् ।
वृक्ष इव स्तब्धो दिवि तिष्ठत्येकस्तेनेदं पूर्णं पुरुषेण सर्वम् ॥ ९

yasmāt param nāparamasti kiñcidyasmānnāṇīyo na jyāyo'sti kaścit |
vrkṣa iva stabdho divi tiṣṭhatyekastenedam pūrṇam puruṣeṇa sarvam
॥ 9

ततो यदुत्तरततं तदरूपमनामयम् ।
य एतद्विदुरमृतास्ते भवन्त्यथेतरे दुःखमेवापियन्ति ॥ १०

tato yaduttaratatam tadarūpamanāmayam | ya
etadviduramṛtāste bhavantyathetare duḥkhamevāpiyanti ॥ 10

यस्मात् than what परं farthest न not अपरम् nearest अस्ति is किञ्चित्
anything यस्मात् than that अणीयः smaller न not ज्यायः bigger
अस्ति is कश्चित् । anything. वृक्षः tree इव like स्तब्धः stationary दिवि
in grandeur तिष्ठति stands एकः the One तेन by Him इदं this पूर्णं
filled पुरुषेण by Being सर्वम् ॥ everything. ततः than यत् what
उत्तरततं highest तत् that अरूपम् formless अन्-आमयम् । without
sorrow. ये those who एतत् this विदुः realize अमृताः untouched
by illness ते they भवन्ति become अथ however इतरे the others
दुःखम् sickness एव only अपियन्ति ॥ incur.

3.9 When we talk of the finer emotion of Rudra like LOVE, we find there isn't anything that stands up to it. Conversely, as LOVE is also soft and weakening, to entice or trap someone there isn't anything better.

When we talk of the fluid nature of Rudra, it becomes apparent that its gigantic waves can knock out an entire galaxy. On the other hand its trickle droplet can seep through the tightest safe and make inroads into the stubborn-nest heart.

Silent motionless too is Rudra, its presence is hence rarely discerned, like a nondescript tree in a forest.

Rudra demands attention from none, it seeks not any company. Stronger than the strongest it cheerfully rests, it feels no need for self-glory.

3.10 Indeed Rudra is in a space unimaginable, its total lack of craving is legendary.

Can you understand this my friend? Can you digest such a Rudra? Can your heart accept and acknowledge such energy? Can your reason not become a hurdle? If so, then know you are close. You are on track.

Else time hangs heavy, else family and friends seem alien, else work is a drag, and life is a burden.

सर्वाननशिरोग्रीवः सर्वभूतगुहाशयः ।
सर्वव्यापी स भगवांस्तस्मात्सर्वगतः शिवः ॥ ११

sarvānanaśirogrīvaḥ sarvabhūtaguhāśayaḥ | sarvavyāpī sa
bhagavāṃstasmātsarvagataḥ śivaḥ ॥ 11

महान्प्रभुर्वै पुरुषः सत्वस्यैष प्रवर्तकः ।
सुनिर्मलामिमां प्राप्तिमीशानो ज्योतिरव्ययः ॥ १२

mahānprabhurvai puruṣaḥ satvasyaiṣa pravartakaḥ |
sunirmalāmimāṃ prāptimīśāno jyotiravyayaḥ ॥ 12

सर्व-आनन-शिरः-ग्रीवः all faces heads necks सर्व-भूत-गुहा-आशयः ।
all beings basic foundation. सर्व-व्यापी omnipresent सः He
भगवान् the Fortune तस्मात् hence सर्व-गतः omniscient शिवः ॥
Shiva the auspicious. महान् wondrous प्रभुः Lord वै indeed पुरुषः
the supreme Self सत्वस्य of the core एषः He प्रवर्तकः । Guide. सु-
निर्-मलाम् shining without stain इमां this प्राप्तिम् enabling ईशानः
the Ruler ज्योतिः the Light अव्ययः ॥ without differentiation.

3.11 In all forms that the eye can see, in all men who walk this planet, know that Rudra is present albeit non-transactable.

All thoughts and all distances are tiny compared to Rudra's domain. His lordly presence and compassionate benevolence are sought for by all, only few make his acquaintance in one lifetime.

3.12 Rudra is hailed by sages as the magnificent indweller of courageous hearts and broad intellects. His light awakens the conscience of man. His presence infuses men with compassion and humility.

RUDRA
- the OIL in all automobiles
- the OJAS in all humans
- the JUICE in vegetables, fruits and nuts
- the CARING faculty in families, societies and nations
- the HEALING quality of medics and medications

अङ्गुष्ठमात्रः पुरुषोऽन्तरात्मा सदा जनानां हृदये सन्निविष्टः ।
हृदा मन्वीशो मनसाऽभिक्लृप्तो य एतद्विदुरमृतास्ते भवन्ति ॥ १३

aṅguṣṭhamātraḥ puruṣo'ntarātmā sadā janānāṃ hṛdaye sanniviṣṭaḥ |
hṛdā manvīśo manasābhiklṛpto ya etadviduramṛtāste bhavanti || 13

अङ्गुष्ठ-मात्रः thumb like पुरुषः the Supreme Being अन्तर्-आत्मा the inner Soul सदा always जनानां of people हृदये in the core सन्निविष्टः । contained. हृदा by deep emotion मन्वीशः fountain of wisdom मनसा by the intellect, imagination, and willpower अभिक्लृप्तः accordingly ये they who एतत् this विदुः recognize अमृताः faultless and incorruptible ते they भवन्ति ॥ are.

3.13 What organ of the body can be used to denote Rudra for purpose of teaching? We can assume the Thumb to represent Rudra, taking into consideration the thumb's size and which can be easily hidden in the fist, its multitasking ability and visible importance.

And where inside the body may we say is Rudra located? It is within one's soul, however since the exact location of the soul is not known, for purpose of teaching we assume it to be in the heart, i.e. the chest center, or the anahata chakra.

How may we know or perceive Rudra?
By a pure हृदा heart, by a clarity of मनसा intellect, by determined will, sincere imagination or ardent prayer it can be felt.

Those brave men who strive with priority and urgency to realize Rudra, attain the superimposition of his will in their day to day life, thus get freed from afflictions.

सहस्रशीर्षा पुरुषः सहस्राक्षः सहस्रपात् ।
स भूमिं विश्वतो वृत्वाऽत्यतिष्ठद्दशाङ्गुलम् ॥ १४

sahasraśīrṣā puruṣaḥ sahasrākṣaḥ sahasrapāt | sa bhūmiṃ viśvato
vṛtvā'tyatiṣṭhaddaśāṅgulam ‖ 14

पुरुष एवेद॰ सर्वं यद्भूतं यच्च भव्यम् ।
उतामृतत्वस्येशानो यदन्नेनातिरोहति ॥ १५

puruṣa eveda(guṃ) sarvaṃ yadbhūtaṃ yacca bhavyam |
utāmṛtatvasyeśāno yadannenātirohati ‖ 15

Famous Verse occurs also in Purusha Suktam verse 1

सहस्र-शीर्षा thousand heads पुरुषः the Supreme Soul सहस्र-अक्षः innumerable eyes सहस्र-पात् । infinite legs. सः He भूमिं the earth विश्वतः completely वृत्वा having covered अत्यतिष्ठत् extends over and above दश-अङ्गुलम् ॥ ten fingers, i.e. much more than anyone can hold in both hands or imagine in the mind. पुरुषः the Divine Being एव only इदं this सर्वं all यद् what भूतं was यद् what च and भव्यम् । shall be. उत verily अमृतत्वस्य of immortality ईशानः the Lord यद् who अन्नेन beyond everything else अति-रोहति ॥ exceedingly grows.

3.14 One may see and feel Rudra in countless day to day experiences. a soft sunrise, a brilliant sunset, the leaves dancing in the breeze.

a loved one's glance, a mother's explosive anger, a sportsman's exhilaration, a student's exceptional examination attempt, someone's witty response.

a stroke of lightning, a raging tornado, a burst of lava that engulfs the town.

Know ye Seeker, Rudra's capability, his ingenuity and inventiveness, his speed and strength, exceed anything that has been observed in the 10 directions, or that can be done by the combined efforts of tens of nations.

3.15 Brahman encompasses Time. What was in the Past, what is in the Present, what shall be in the Future, are all within Brahman's preview.

It may appear that parts of him in the form of body and matter are destructible, and that his energies are transformable, it is all just his play. Unaffected is he, it is all just his prank, his style of entertainment are all these names and forms we see.

सर्वतःपाणिपादं तत् सर्वतोऽक्षिशिरोमुखम् ।
सर्वतः श्रुतिमल्लोके सर्वमावृत्य तिष्ठति ॥ १६

sarvataḥpāṇipādaṃ tat sarvato'kṣiśiromukham |

sarvataḥśrutimalloke sarvamāvṛtya tiṣṭhati ॥ 16

सर्वेन्द्रियगुणाभासं सर्वेन्द्रियविवर्जितम् ।
सर्वस्य प्रभुमीशानं सर्वस्य शरणं बृहत् ॥ १७

sarvendriyaguṇābhāsaṃ sarvendriyavivarjitam | sarvasya

prabhumīśānaṃ sarvasya śaraṇaṃ bṛhat ॥ 17

सर्वतःपाणि-पादं everywhere hands and feet तत् it सर्वतः all enveloping अक्षि-शिरो-मुखम् । eyes heads mouths सर्वतः all sides श्रुतिमत् hearing ears लोके in cosmos सर्वम् all आवृत्य covering तिष्ठति ॥ exists. सर्व-इन्द्रिय-गुण-आभासं all sensory qualities functional सर्व-इन्द्रिय-विवर्जितम् । any sense cannot grasp सर्वस्य of all प्रभुम् the Lord ईशानं the loving Guide सर्वस्य of each शरणं the refuge बृहत् ॥ significant.

3.16 To the devotee, to the bhakta, to the enlightened Master, all the hands that act are doing his bidding, all the feet that walk are walking towards him.

All the beautiful eyes search for him, all the clashing egos announce his pranks, all the handsome faces reflect his glory.

All ears strain to catch his word, all efforts are done to please him alone.

3.17 When senses get purified through the practice of Brahmacharya celibacy, they turn inwards and seek him, they glimpse him and revel in him.

The intellect then acknowledges him as the Boss, the Idol, the Refuge and the best friend.

नवद्वारे पुरे देही हꣳसो लेलायते बहिः ।
वशी सर्वस्य लोकस्य स्थावरस्य चरस्य च ॥ १८

navadvāre pure dehī haṃso lelāyate bahiḥ | vaśī sarvasya lokasya
sthāvarasya carasya ca || 18

अपाणिपादो जवनो ग्रहीता पश्यत्यचक्षुः स श्रृणोत्यकर्णः ।
स वेत्ति वेद्यं न च तस्यास्ति वेत्ता तमाहुरग्र्यं पुरुषं महान्तम् ॥ १९

apāṇipādo javano grahītā paśyatyacakṣuḥ sa śṛṇotyakarṇaḥ | sa
vetti vedyaṃ na ca tasyāsti vettā tamāhuragryaṃ puruṣaṃ
mahāntam || 19

नव-द्वारे of nine gates पुरे in the bodily city देही inside the body
हंसः the swan like pure soul लेलायते happily plays बहिः ।
outside. वशी king सर्वस्य whole लोकस्य world's स्थावरस्य
inanimate stationary चरस्य animate expressing च ॥ and. अ-
पाणि-पादः not needing help nor vehicle जवनः swiftly ग्रहीता the
Knower पश्यति sees अ-चक्षुः without external eyes सः He श्रृणोति
hears अ-कर्णः । minus sensory ears. सः He वेत्ति knows वेद्यं
whatever is to be known न none च and तस्य of Him अस्ति is
वेत्ता knower तम् Him आहुः they declare अग्र्यं foremost पुरुषं Man
महान्तम् ॥ most superior.

3.18 The human body has nine exits (2 eyes, 2 ears, nose, mouth, navel, bum, and penis). Each is an entry and exit for Brahman. Each such frame with a capable nervous system can house him and make him welcome.

The pure Swan (an epithet for Brahman as it can separate milk from a watery mix), glides forth and evokes the desire to be free in man. Only men with Viveka and Vairagya discern the graceful Swan or have a glimpse of Brahman.

The rest continue as bound mechanical beings, unduly tied to work and family, overly tied to societal obligations, and never for a moment wish to know Him.

3.19 He has no need for anatomical hands, nor for mechanical feet. His will accomplishes all, by will alone He moves.

Nor does He require sensory eyes or ears or fancy gadgets, His means of information are simply a matter of will.

He can fathom any design and thought, no plans escape His keenness. Only an awakened being can sense Him.

It has been declared by the Enlightened Masters - "Who came First is He, Who is a perfect man is He, Who is Gigantic and Magnificent is He".

अणोरणीयान्महतो महीयानात्मा गुहायां निहितोऽस्य जन्तोः ।
तमक्रतुः पश्यति वीतशोको धातुः प्रसादान्महिमानमीशम् ॥ २०

aṇoraṇīyānmahato mahīyānātmā guhāyāṃ nihito'sya jantoḥ ।
tamakratuḥ paśyati vītaśoko dhātuḥ prasādānmahimānamīśam ॥ 20

वेदाहमेतमजरं पुराणं सर्वात्मानं सर्वगतं विभुत्वात् ।
जन्मनिरोधं प्रवदन्ति यस्य ब्रह्मवादिनो हि प्रवदन्ति नित्यम् ॥ २१

vedāhametamajaraṃ purāṇaṃ sarvātmānaṃ sarvagataṃ vibhutvāt । janmanirodhaṃ pravadanti yasya brahmavādino hi pravadanti nityam ॥ 21

अणोः than an atom अणीयान् smaller महतः than the greatest महीयान् greater आत्मा the pure Soul गुहायां in the deepest part निहितः hidden अस्य is जन्तोः । of a creature.
तम् Him अ-क्रतुः non-feverishness पश्यति sees वीत-शोकः free of suffering धातुः primal substance प्रसादात् from grace महिमानम् the Famed ईशम् ॥ Lord. वेद know अहम् i एतम् Him who is so close अजरं undecaying पुराणं ancient yet ever relevant सर्व-आत्मानं omniscient सर्व-गतं omnipresent विभुत्वात् । due to omnipotence. जन्म-निरोधं प्रवदन्ति they the wise say यस्य whose ब्रह्म-वादिनः Brahman knowers हि indeed प्रवदन्ति the saints say नित्यम् ॥ always.

3.20 Brahman is fluid and can pass through the smallest atom and influence its spin bypassing any nearby atoms. It can make a single strand of hair lustrous by raising its vitamin levels. It can penetrate deep into the intellect and clear finicky notions.

Brahman is vast and can affect the destiny of entire galactic phenomena. It can infuse any team with the spirit to win the Olympic gold or rule over the World.

A man's heart is the place where it is supposed to be concealed, albeit only in the purer and innocent beings it houses itself.

The brave and the modest are blessed with its grace, the pure souls experience its working, and shorn of covetousness they transcend the plane of heartburn and pain.

3.21 O how fortunate am i to have been blessed by the darshan of the Lord. i feel His presence, i experience His glory, i know He is eternal and that He is my root cause.

i realize He moves in all beings at will, i sense Him in nature and in family, friends, neighbors, also in strangers.

The Sages declare Him to be causeless. The knowers of Brahman declare It to be ever available, always helpful, ready to support the greatest ventures, and lend a hand to the boldest move and the classiest thought.

4th Teaching (manifest Brahman)

Necessity of Faith

चतुर्थोऽध्यायः
य एकोऽवर्णो बहुधा शक्तियोगाद्वर्णाननेकान्निहितार्थो दधाति ।
वि चैति चान्ते विश्वमादौ स देवः स नो बुद्ध्या शुभया संयुनक्तु ॥ १

caturtho'dhyāyaḥ
ya eko'varṇo bahudhā śaktiyogādvarṇānanekānnihitārtho dadhāti | vi caiti cānte viśvamādau sa devaḥ sa no buddhyā śubhayā saṃyunaktu ॥ 1

4.1 He is a well-integrated composite being with innumerable skills at his command. His chief vocation is to create various things and engineer different phenomena. He enjoys a diversity of flora and fauna. He produces various religions, tenets, and dictums, and takes many births to follow and apply one or another practice.

Each practice may be polarized wrt another, each practice may have certain common traits and few vastly different precepts.

May he enlighten the powerful nations so that at least some are able to transcend the differences and revel in the polarity. A melting pot of ideas, a soup of vegetables from far lands, and a mixing of languages and cultures to whom he blesses with, are the most fortunate folk.

तदेवाग्निस्तदादित्यस्तद्वायुस्तदु चन्द्रमाः ।
तदेव शुक्रं तद्ब्रह्म तदापस्तत्प्रजापतिः ॥ २

tadevāgnistadādityastadvāyustadu candramāḥ | tadeva śukraṃ
tadbrahma tadāpastatprajāpatiḥ || 2

त्वं स्त्री त्वं पुमानसि त्वं कुमार उत वा कुमारी ।
त्वं जीर्णो दण्डेन वञ्चसि त्वं जातो भवसि विश्वतोमुखः ॥ ३

tvaṃ strī tvaṃ pumānasi tvaṃ kumāra uta vā kumārī | tvaṃ jīrṇo
daṇḍena vañcasi tvaṃ jāto bhavasi viśvatomukhaḥ || 3

4.2 May the powers that be see the same Fire is used for cooking in all homes, and the same Sun at dawn greets all the lands.

The same Air is breathed in and circulated in and out of each nose on the planet.

All men use the same Moon to woo their beloved, all lovers enjoy the one moonlight streaming on earth and romantic Venus to aid their marriages.

The Wisdom in each culture speaks of tolerance, forbearance, sharing and caring.

Waters everywhere quench parched throats and delight the soul.

Farmers Teachers Doctors and Engineers all do the same thing irrespective of language, culture, affiliation or economic status.

4.3 Each Girl and every Boy, whether baby, teen, adult or senior, loves to interact, communicate and exchange.

Excitement erupts on distant meetings of old comrades, friends are thrilled when a long lost face shows up.

Virgins may get involved with oldies, the poor boy may entice the wealthy girl.

It's not a mystery, it's nothing new. Only you the director pulling the strings and arranging the sets.

नीलः पतङ्गो हरितो लोहिताक्षस्तडिद्गर्भ ऋतवः समुद्राः ।
अनादिमत्त्वं विभुत्वेन वर्तसे यतो जातानि भुवनानि विश्वा ॥ ४

nīlaḥ pataṅgo harito lohitākṣastaḍidgarbha ṛtavaḥ samudrāḥ |
anādimattvaṃ vibhutvena vartase yato jātāni bhuvanāni viśvā ‖ 4

अजामेकां लोहितशुक्लकृष्णां बह्वीः प्रजाः सृजमानां सरूपाः ।
अजो ह्येको जुषमाणोऽनुशेते जहात्येनां भुक्तभोगामजोऽन्यः ॥ ५

ajāmekāṃ lohitaśuklakṛṣṇāṃ bahvīḥ prajāḥ sṛjamānāṃ sarūpāḥ |
ajo hyeko juṣamāṇo'nuśete jahātyenāṃ bhuktabhogāmajo'nyaḥ ‖
5

4.4 Thou art the blue butterfly, the green hued parrot sporting inquisitive red eyes.

Thou light up the scenery with lightning flashes accompanied with booming thunder from ominous dark clouds.

You cause seasons to unfurl and put up a heroic show every two months, you make the seas teem with millions of salmon, sharks, whales and dolphins.

You cannot be framed in a picture, you cannot be justified by words, it is hard to pinpoint your beginnings if any.

What is sure is that you make us all experience the highest pleasure, you ensure that all beings have their say, their day, and hog the limelight once in a lifetime.

4.5 Uncaused unmade unruled, your energy branches into luminous sattva, energetic rajas, and balancing tamas.

Like a magician's mathematics, the branched energies recombine to produce non-quantifiable, unaccounted for and uncountable beings.

When or how anyone dies or anything destroys is never stated, it seems this is also an incredible law, albeit it satisfies and satiates all.

द्वा सुपर्णा सयुजा सखाया समानं वृक्षं परिषस्वजाते ।
तयोरन्यः पिप्पलं स्वाद्वत्त्यनश्नन्नन्यो अभिचाकशीति ॥ ६

dvā suparṇā sayujā sakhāyā samānaṃ vṛkṣaṃ pariṣasvajāte |
tayoranyaḥ pippalaṃ svādvattyanaśnannanyo abhicākaśīti ॥ 6

4.6 O look at myself. Am i not the two, the mind and the soul?

Look at my sturdy frame and handsome features, look at my wealth and my beautiful companions.

Q. Who is looking and enjoying all this? A. Obviously the MIND. The ticking clock in me, the stream of thoughts, the decision maker MIND sitting in the body is experiencing all of it just like a dove sitting on a tree, pecking at berries.

Q. What about the SOUL? A . O it's calmly watching the spectacle, wondering when the MIND shall look up to it. Certainly that is going to take a long time and many events later only shall the MIND get tired of its shallow living. After it is fully spent, then alone the racing MIND drops and looks up and spots the unperturbed SOUL. Just as the dove looks up and spots its mate only after it's finished with its mundane chore.

समाने वृक्षे पुरुषो निमग्नोऽनीशया शोचति मुह्यमानः ।
जुष्टं यदा पश्यत्यन्यमीशमस्य महिमानमिति वीतशोकः ॥ ७

samāne vṛkṣe puruṣo nimagno'nīśayā śocati muhyamānaḥ |
juṣṭaṃ yadā paśyatyanyamīśamasya mahimānamiti vītaśokaḥ || 7

4.7 The MIND due to its feverish hankering keeps running hither and tither, then by some grace it gets the SOUL's darshan. One look at the SOUL, one glance by the SOUL, and the MIND understands in a flash that the Captain loves it, the Commander is at its side, the Big Boss is its bosom friend and well-wisher.

In that instant the MIND is freed. In that instant it unites with the SOUL, dropping all pent up emotions, clearing all backlog.

In a flash understanding dawns - the entire creation is for it solely, all wealth in the creation belongs to it alone, there is none but itself there.

This is what Satsang does. Singing together, chanting together, praying together, listening to the Master's discourse, they all lead to this awakening.

ऋचो अक्षरे परमे व्योमन्यस्मिन्देवा अधि विश्वे निषेदुः ।
यस्तं न वेद किमृचा करिष्यति य इत्तद्विदुस्त इमे समासते ॥ ८

ṛco akṣare parame vyomanyasmindevā adhi viśve niṣeduḥ ।
yastaṃ na veda kimṛcā kariṣyati ya ittadvidusta ime samāsate ॥ 8

4.8 O of what use is any discipline or practice or ritual if it does not accept all and honor all and fails to see the oneness in all?

O what of dictums or tenets that discriminate based on the skin color or cloth or style of worship or language?

O Brahman can the narrow minded highly differentiated specimens ever glimpse thee? May you allow them also the benefit of grace in a moment of compassion?

So many learned scholars profess one-sided opinions and live biased lives, so many nations enforce one law to fit all.

Never mind, the verses uttered by a Master can cleave and heal, his compassion can destroy the pockets of stubbornness. Pray someone can get initiation by an enlightened master, and the veil of ignorance is torn asunder.

छन्दांसि यज्ञाः क्रतवो व्रतानि भूतं भव्यं यच्च वेदा वदन्ति ।
अस्मान्मायी सृजते विश्वमेतत्तस्मिंश्चान्यो मायया सन्निरुद्धः ॥ ९

chandāṃsi yajñāḥ kratavo vratāni bhūtaṃ bhavyaṃ yacca vedā
vadanti | asmānmāyī sṛjate viśvametattasmiṃścānyo māyayā
sanniruddhaḥ || 9

4.9 O how beautiful! O what a wonder.

O how is it possible, how is it done?

A part of thee (MIND) is so confused, a part of thee (SOUL) is so clear.

A part of thee is the Lord and a part of thee is the SLAVE. Is that the way to produce merriment? Is that a common law for entertainment?

Perhaps contrast gives rise to pleasure, perhaps the up after a down is really something.

Time and again the scriptures say - if you wish to unite in yoga, then have a discipline of havan, satsang and celibacy.

Have a control over sleep, food, and entertainment. And paths will open for you to walk free, paths will open and lead you to bliss.

And what of those who are wayward and lethargic. Well they keep spinning endlessly like tops, tightly bound, almost imprisoned.

मायां तु प्रकृतिं विद्यान्मायिनं च महेश्वरम् ।
तस्यावयवभूतैस्तु व्याप्तं सर्वमिदं जगत् ॥ १०

māyāṃ tu prakṛtiṃ vidyānmāyinaṃ ca maheśvaram |
tasyāvayavabhūtaistu vyāptaṃ sarvamidaṃ jagat ॥ 10

यो योनिं योनिमधितिष्ठत्येको यस्मिन्निदं सं च वि चैति सर्वम् ।
तमीशानं वरदं देवमीड्यं निचाय्येमां शान्तिमत्यन्तमेति ॥ ११

yo yoniṃ yonimadhitiṣṭhatyeko yasminnidaṃ saṃ ca vi caiti
sarvam | tamīśānaṃ varadaṃ devamīḍyaṃ nicāyyemāṃ
śāntimatyantameti ॥ 11

4.10 Ok, so it means both the true and the false coexist in creation.

Truth is that which stands firm under trying circumstances, falsehood crumbles when faced with inquisition.

The great Lord allows both, and all combinations of principles as well. It is up to you to choose your inclination, and then follow your gut feeling to the end. Whenever in doubt, know that Truth triumphs, albeit in the end.

This is where discipline comes in. Discipline ensures you do not give up or give in, it helps keep you on track, and it makes the difficult times pass by without scar.

4.11 Understand it well. The good Lord manifests infinity in the physical and practical domain.

What does this mean? Does it mean that the same Lord who is glorified as the best and strongest and swiftest, also shows up as the middling or the worse, the weak or the hypocrite, the lame or the lethargic?

Be very careful. Now stop and remove all bias and notion.

The same Lord who is prayed to by all and who is the support and fountain of bliss, also reflects as this mundane creation with all its bile and humor. The physical beings and human gadgets and endeavors and manmade laws, all derive their identity, their current, their half-life and their impact from the same strand of pure divinity. The emotional turbulences and the terrible storms are all powered by the one source.

Does that mean that God is mean or temperamental or stupid. Not at all. Do not go on this track, since it shall only lead to your own downfall and pain.

Then how to use or interpret the Lord's infinite nature? It must be awakened and assimilated within oneself that even though right is right and wrong is wrong, still one cannot do wrong against wrong.

The teaching is given to prevent the seed of hatred, bitterness, non-forgiveness, rigidity, or guile from taking root. When an ignorant man commits a blunder, to save one's inherent innocence, one must attribute the incident to the mysterious ways of the Lord, rather than attaching blame on a person, gadget, institution or nation.

The one who can see beyond a localized event, sees the great lord's affable smile, and is freed from limiting prejudice, is freed from karmic impressions, and is able to perform to optimum potential and live a really cool life.

यो देवानां प्रभवश्चोद्भवश्च विश्वाधिपो रुद्रो महर्षिः ।
हिरण्यगर्भं पश्यत जायमानं स नो बुद्ध्या शुभया संयुनक्तु ॥ १२

yo devānāṃ prabhavaścodbhavaśca viśvādhipo rudro maharṣiḥ |
hiraṇyagarbhaṃ paśyata jāyamānaṃ sa no buddhyā śubhayā
saṃyunaktu || 12

यो देवानामधिपो यस्मिँल्लोका अधिश्रिताः ।
य ईशे अस्य द्विपदश्चतुष्पदः कस्मै देवाय हविषा विधेम ॥ १३

yo devānāmadhipo yasmiṃllokā adhiśritāḥ | ya īśe asya
dvipadaścatuṣpadaḥ kasmai devāya haviṣā vidhema || 13

सूक्ष्मातिसूक्ष्मं कलिलस्य मध्ये विश्वस्य स्रष्टारमनेकरूपम् ।
विश्वस्यैकं परिवेष्टितारं ज्ञात्वा शिवं शान्तिमत्यन्तमेति ॥ १४

sūkṣmātisūkṣmaṃ kalilasya madhye viśvasya
sraṣṭhāramanekarūpam | viśvasyaikaṃ pariveṣṭitāraṃ jñātvā
śivaṃ śāntimatyantameti || 14

4.12 O almighty! May we hark to thy teaching and heed thy word. May our bias and notion be fluid and our memory be clear.

May we walk calmly, courageously, and with ample faith.

4.13 May we sing thy glory, may we relate heroic stories to grandchildren.

May we take out time to welcome the physical God FIRE, by lighting lamps, doing havan along with cheering, clapping and singing.

4.14 O heaven! May we strive to see the sliver of grace in the gloomy cloud, may we acknowledge thy hand in our failure and so do inner contemplation.

May we see the pro in every con, may we enhance our skill and broaden our vision to lend a helping hand.

स एव काले भुवनस्य गोप्ता विश्वाधिपः सर्वभूतेषु गूढः ।
यस्मिन्युक्ता ब्रह्मर्षयो देवताश्च तमेवं ज्ञात्वा मृत्युपाशांश्छिनत्ति ॥ १५

sa eva kāle bhuvanasya goptā viśvādhipaḥ sarvabhūteṣu gūḍhaḥ |
yasminyuktā brahmarṣayo devatāśca tamevaṃ jñātvā
mṛtyupāśāṃśchinatti ‖ 15

घृतात्परं मण्डमिवातिसूक्ष्मं ज्ञात्वा शिवं सर्वभूतेषु गूढम् ।
विश्वस्यैकं परिवेष्टितारं ज्ञात्वा देवं मुच्यते सर्वपाशैः ॥ १६

ghṛtātparaṃ maṇḍamivātisūkṣmaṃ jñātvā śivaṃ sarvabhūteṣu
gūḍham | viśvasyaikaṃ pariveṣṭitāraṃ jñātvā devaṃ mucyate
sarvapāśaiḥ ‖ 16

4.15 O Brahman! May we understand the contradiction that even though all are thee, yet thee never are where wickedness brews.

Thee are not at all aware of the cruel demonic currents that surface once in a while, since thee are far far away. Thee are fast asleep and curled up in a furry ball, oblivious to the tyrannical events unfolding.

Thee manifest in your effulgent ignorance annihilating light only in particular modes of time space combinations. You remain unperturbed, hidden it is said, till the very last.

Hence the sages introduce the concept of Vastu to welcome thee while constructing homes and temples, and honor the Shivaratri and Navaratri as being times of your abundant availability.

4.16 You arise within minds at will, you visit when one is totally unsuspecting, your prick to the conscience is felt only by the soft heart.

Hence we say that guests are gods, hence we say that strangers can be saviors.

एष देवो विश्वकर्मा महात्मा सदा जनानां हृदये सन्निविष्टः ।
हृदा मनीषा मनसाभिक्लृप्तो य एतद्विदुरमृतास्ते भवन्ति ॥ १७

eṣa devo viśvakarmā mahātmā sadā janānāṃ hṛdaye sanniviṣṭaḥ |
hṛdā manīṣā manasābhiklṛpto ya etadviduramṛtāste bhavanti ‖ 17

यदाऽतमस्तान्न दिवा न रात्रिर्न सन्न चासच्छिव एव केवलः ।
तदक्षरं तत्सवितुर्वरेण्यं प्रज्ञा च तस्मात्प्रसृता पुराणी ॥ १८

yadā'tamastānna divā na rātrirna sanna cāsacchiva eva kevalaḥ |
tadakṣaraṃ tatsaviturvareṇyaṃ prajñā ca tasmātprasṛtā purāṇī ‖
18

4.17 Only a gentle heart can accommodate your generous frame, a tight mind is unable to let you in.

You rub like sandpaper against the blunt and sharp emotions, you tear down narrow intellects and bulldoze crowded neural streets, such men shudder to give you passage.

The Upanishads call you as - not this, not that, not anything else either, so that men may not cage you or idolize only a particular form of yours.

The Upanishads describe you as everything, as nothing, as neither of the two, as both simultaneously, and also as that which the intellect cannot reason out, nor the senses can grasp.

Please may we not hang on to picture frames or banana skins, may we not make assumptions regarding a coconut without ever opening it and looking in.

4.18 May we understand that weekdays and weekends are societal constructs, may we understand that religions and cultures are time space dependent.

May we not label day as good or night as bad, may we not fall prey to notions of my family alone is royal or needy.

May we not enforce laws without listening to the presence, may we not go on mob fury due to misguided elders. May the early Sunlight be our rudder, may the wisdom of Sages be our raft.

नैनमूर्ध्वं न तिर्यञ्चं न मध्ये न परिजग्रभत् ।
न तस्य प्रतिमा अस्ति यस्य नाम महद्यशः ॥ १९

nainamūrdhvaṃ na tiryañcaṃ na madhye na parijagrabhat | na
tasya pratimā asti yasya nāma mahadyaśaḥ || 19

92

न संदृशे तिष्ठति रूपमस्य न चक्षुषा पश्यति कश्चनैनम् ।
हृदा हृदिस्थं मनसा य एन-मेवं विदुरमृतास्ते भवन्ति ॥ २०

na saṃdṛśe tiṣṭhati rūpamasya na cakṣuṣā paśyati kaścanainam |
hṛdā hṛdisthaṃ manasā ya ena-mevaṃ viduramṛtāste bhavanti || 20

4.19 Please may we not think we alone have realized Him, may we not strut about in enlightenment.

No idols, nay no definition of God can light a candle unto Him.

He that is Great is gigantic and unknown, fine and invisible.

4.20 We make many pictures and idols and yantras of Him, we worship Him by different names and forms and rituals.

Each belief and each method is sufficient to reach Him, though none can be said to be exclusive.

Each path and all names lead to Him, never for a moment claim your path is superior.

अजात इत्येवं कश्चिद्भीरुः प्रपद्यते ।

रुद्र यत्ते दक्षिणं मुखं तेन मां पाहि नित्यम् ॥ २१

ajāta ityevaṃ kaścidbhīruḥ prapadyate | rudra yatte dakṣiṇaṃ
mukhaṃ tena māṃ pāhi nityam || 21

मा नस्तोके तनये मा न आयुषि मा नो गोषु मा न अश्वेषु रीरिषः ।

वीरान् मा नो रुद्र भामितो वधीर्हविष्मन्तः सदामित् त्वा हवामहे ॥ २२

mā nastoke tanaye mā na āyuṣi mā no goṣu mā na aśveṣu rīriṣaḥ |
vīrān mā no rudra bhāmito vadhīrhaviṣmantaḥ sadāmit tvā
havāmahe || 22

4.21 Seasons are sinusoidal, Nature is cyclic, history repeats itself.

How may we say 'this is the start and that is the end'?

Whichever time and season is now, may we welcome thee forthwith without losing the opportunity.

May we make you the priority, may we run to join the kindness wagon, sing lustily, and dance to our heart's content.

4.22 O Divine Lord Rudra! May we enjoy the togetherness of Rudra abhisheka. May our children and grandchildren and neighbors not miss this rare bounty.

May we not be stuck in other activity in our mind during Abhisheka. If we cannot help the proceedings or be in awe of the spectacle, may we simply close our eyes and be lost in meditation.

O Rudra! It is a great fortune to partake of your divine glory in puja, to organize a puja, or to simply invite near and dear ones to the puja.

5th Teaching (living the Brahman)

Transactional aspect of Brahman

<u>पञ्चमोध्यायः</u>

द्वे अक्षरे ब्रह्मपरे त्वनन्ते विद्याविद्ये निहिते यत्र गूढे ।

क्षरं त्वविद्या ह्यमृतं तु विद्या विद्याविद्ये ईशते यस्तु सोऽन्यः ॥ १

pañcamodhyāyaḥ

dve akṣare brahmapare tvanante vidyāvidye nihite yatra gūḍhe |

kṣaraṃ tvavidyā hyamṛtaṃ tu vidyā vidyāvidye īśate yastu so'nyaḥ

‖ 1

यो योनिं योनिमधितिष्ठत्येको विश्वानि रूपाणि योनीश्च सर्वाः ।

ऋषिं प्रसूतं कपिलं यस्तमग्रे ज्ञानैर्बिभर्ति जायमानं च पश्येत् ॥ २

yo yoniṃ yonimadhitiṣṭhatyeko viśvāni rūpāṇi yonīśca sarvāḥ |

ṛṣiṃ prasūtaṃ kapilaṃ yastamagre jñānairbibharti jāyamānaṃ ca

paśyet ‖ 2

5.1 Brahman is said to be dual. The infinite when it starts to transact, divides itself in small finite pieces so that a dialog and a play can be enacted.

In this movie, the protagonist and the antagonist both get prominent roles. The hidden heroine is the prize, both vie for her, forgetting that the real hero is within.

Brahman watches the play nonplussed. We cannot say that he takes either side. The hero goes on to prove himself worthy, the villain chooses to make himself detested.

5.2 When prayers happen, when there is non-feverish worship, He takes birth as happy and strong children, or as blooming flowers and luscious fruit, or even as diamond and mineral ore.

He becomes the elements of the periodic table and the disciplines of university study, and also the inventions and discoveries.

एकैक जालं बहुधा विकुर्वन्नस्मिन्क्षेत्रे संहरत्येष देवः ।
भूयः सृष्ट्वा पतयस्तथेशः सर्वाधिपत्यं कुरुते महात्मा ॥ ३

ekaika jālaṃ bahudhā vikurvannasminkṣetre saṃharatyeṣa devaḥ |
bhūyaḥ sṛṣṭvā patayastatheśaḥ sarvādhipatyaṃ kurute mahātmā ॥ 3

सर्वा दिश ऊर्ध्वमधश्च तिर्यक्प्रकाशयन्त्राजते यद्वनड्वान् ।
एवं स देवो भगवान्वरेण्यो योनिस्वभावानधितिष्ठत्येकः ॥ ४

sarvā diśa ūrdhvamadhaśca tiryak prakāśayanbhrājate
yadvanaḍvān | evaṃ sa devo bhagavānvareṇyo
yonisvabhāvānadhitiṣṭhatyekaḥ ॥ 4

5.3 One set of laws is made to usher in the Satyug, another set proves to be Kalyug.

Even though spaced out in time, the laws get superseded by the earnest devotees, and for them the laws yield with glee.

Some say the laws are permanent, others acknowledge their impermanence. Both however agree on the supremacy of Brahman, both seek Him alone.

5.4 All homes are lit by the morning sunlight, all fires glow by the same principle.

All smiles arouse and excite, all fruits wish to be plucked.

The credit goes to Him, He chooses to become the exciter, the nourisher, and the Attraction.

यच्च स्वभावं पचति विश्वयोनिः पाच्यांश्च सर्वान्परिणामयेद्यः ।
सर्वमेतद्विश्वमधितिष्ठत्येको गुणांश्च सर्वान्विनियोजयेद् यः ॥ ५

yacca svabhāvaṃ pacati viśvayoniḥ pācyāṃśca
sarvānpariṇāmayedyaḥ | sarvametadviśvamadhitiṣṭhatyeko
guṇāṃśca sarvānviniyojayed yaḥ || 5

तद्वेदगुह्योपनिषत्सु गूढं तद्ब्रह्मा वेदते ब्रह्मयोनिम् ।
ये पूर्वंदेवा ऋषयश्च तद्विदुस्ते तन्मया अमृता वै बभूवुः ॥ ६

tadvedaguhyopaniṣatsu gūḍhaṃ tadbrahmā vedate brahmayonim
| ye pūrvaṃdevā ṛṣayaśca tadviduste tanmayā amṛtā vai
babhūvuḥ || 6

5.5 He doesn't lift a finger, His presence alone causes all flutter and hustle and bustle.

He doesn't will anything, yet all laws seek his approval and praise. Gravity, electricity, love and excitement, all hope to please Him.

The three states of matter, the three divisions of time, the three components of every atom, grandfather father and son, all function by His grace, all sway to His wave.

5.6 And what is this esoteric teaching that is available to the earnest and sincere? That gets revealed within by yogic discipline?

That is not understood by temple preaching or hasty ritual? That can take more than a lifetime of persistent enquiry?

The Upanishad says, first open your door wide, remove bias, clean your memory. Be available to accept a living Master in the present. Do not close the door of the intellect based on past principle. Do not live 500 years in historical context. Your mind is new, your clothes are new, your tongue is new and your wife is new.

Sit in Satsang, absorb the Master's words through each pore. Maintain discipline in eating and entertainment. Slowly the haze over Brahman thins, the mist clears and the Lord is experienced.

गुणान्वयो यः फलकर्मकर्ता कृतस्य तस्यैव स चोपभोक्ता ।
स विश्वरूपस्त्रिगुणस्त्रिवर्त्मा प्राणाधिपः संचरति स्वकर्मभिः ॥ ७

guṇānvayo yaḥ phalakarmakartā kṛtasya tasyaiva sa copabhoktā |
sa viśvarūpastriguṇastrivartmā prāṇādhipaḥ saṃcarati
svakarmabhiḥ ॥ 7

5.7 Brahman dispenses the fruits to the sincere seeker, who is living in balance and intensely longing for bliss.

Brahman designs situations and creates platforms for individuals according to their capacity and inclination.

Brahman moves softly and silently unknown and unnoticed. He rejoices with the happy, and ignores those too entangled.

His mighty triad of Sattva Rajas Tamas creates innumerable phenomena to keep all beings and all things fully occupied.

Even though most beings and things ultimately dissolve in the Lord, the ones who follow an equation of 40% sattva 40% rajas and 20% tamas cross the finishing line quicker.

And what are the three aims each particle of matter and each wavelet of energy strives for?
Having good company, (Love)
Being able to express freely, (Acceptance)
Shining in at least one virtue. (Pride)

अङ्गुष्ठमात्रो रवितुल्यरूपः सङ्कल्पाहङ्कारसमन्वितो यः ।
बुद्धेर्गुणेनात्मगुणेन चैव आराग्रमात्रो ह्यपरोऽपि दृष्टः ॥ ८

aṅguṣṭhamātro ravitulyarūpaḥ saṅkalpāhaṅkārasamanvito yaḥ |
buddherguṇenātmaguṇena caiva ārāgramātro hyaparo'pi dṛṣṭaḥ ||
8

5.8 Thumb is the easiest example that comes to mind when we need to express the inexpressible.

We all have a thumb and know it is indispensable in day to day work. We express self-identity by showing the thumb. The toy soldiers, cars and animals that children play with, are made thumb size too.

The Upanishad says that the soul inside us is thumb size. Its throne is placed in the region of the heart, or the center of the chest, and this is said just for conveying the idea that the soul is the boss and is centrally located.

Further it is stated that the soul shines brilliantly, to mean that it is pure divinity, and also to mean that each particle of creation is infused with Brahman.

Now what does a soul within a body Lord over? Naturally the soul shall play the part suited to its body. Just as in a fancy dress competition, the child who becomes a milkmaid acts like her, the one who becomes a tiger roars and growls, the one who becomes a motorcycle zooms past.

Similarly, seeing its body, the soul acts accordingly. If it is a flute, it plays soothing notes, if it is a scorpion it bites, if it is a saint it heals, and if it is salt it makes food tasty.

Here one additional point is to be understood. In the body of anything else except man, the traits of the body are well known and largely without exception. However in the body of man, it is so decreed that one may play any role. Man's nervous system has been so designed that it can express infinity, or it can express any particle or idea of creation.

Thus we learn that buddhi or reason may accept the body and perform accordingly, or it may very well set out to do the unthinkable and the incredible.

A cobbler's awl is mentioned to indicate that the soul takes a body - by means of a sperm that is shaped like an awl,
- the soul like an awl can drill holes and guide the stitch, i.e. it can guide the reason to take proper decisions. It also means that blocked intellects simply need a bit of piercing just as ear piercing transforms the personality
- proper shoes should be a high priority item and must be carefully chosen to suit one's personality and role, apart from being comfortable and functional.
- the shoe is a symbol of movement or evolution of soul.

बालाग्रशतभागस्य शतधा कल्पितस्य च ।
भागो जीवः स विज्ञेयः स चानन्त्याय कल्पते ॥ ९

bālāgraśatabhāgasya śatadhā kalpitasya ca | bhāgo jīvaḥ sa vijñeyaḥ sa cānantyāya kalpate ॥ 9

5.9 Now to remove any notion of size or color or shape that the student may visualize as being the soul, it is stated that the actual size of the soul is finer than a hair split ten thousand times.

I.e. the pure divinity within man is practically invisible, and we should not give it any color or shape that our senses can grasp. Hence a particular form or idol of God is not the only one, any other ideology giving another form must be equally acceptable.

The Upanishad goes on to say that the pure divine soul is always aiming to merge into the infinite purity, i.e. like a sunray it has the potential to withdraw backwards into the sun.

नैव स्त्री न पुमानेष न चैवायं नपुंसकः ।
यद्यच्छरीरमादत्ते तेने तेने स युज्यते ॥ १०

naiva strī na pumāneṣa na caivāyaṃ napuṃsakaḥ |
yadyaccharīramādatte tene tene sa yujyate ॥ 10

सङ्कल्पनस्पर्शनदृष्टिमोहैर्ग्रासांबुवृष्ट्या चत्मविवृद्धिजन्म ।
कर्मानुगान्यनुक्रमेण देही स्थानेषु रूपाण्यभिसम्प्रपद्यते ॥ ११

saṅkalpanasparśanadṛṣṭimohairgrāsāṃbuvṛṣṭyā
catmavivṛddhijanma | karmānugānyanukrameṇa dehī sthāneṣu
rūpāṇyabhisamprapadyate ॥ 11

5.10 The soul is not tied to a woman's body at all times, the soul is also reborn as a man.

The soul is not confined to humans alone, it manifests in every gadget, thing, herb, medicine, home, religion, principle, flower or photon as well.

5.11 The embodied soul evolves into a new body or a higher plane with each successive birth.

It directs the intellect at times, at other times when it has gone out of the body, the intellect runs on auto pilot, and is much prone to error. The soul thus enjoys a managed and an unmanaged tenure, since by nature it is neither tied to the body, nor does a particular body fascinate it more.

The rare Master understands this inherently, and rarely does the soul take a Masterly body.

In other words there are innumerable body choices in the non-living and living spectrum, and the soul doesn't particularly favor any.

The Brahman is present in various bodies as individual souls. Each soul has differing levels of brightness or amplitude. Like a stream has tributaries, like the electric supply has different wattages in each household.

स्थूलानि सूक्ष्माणि बहूनि चैव रूपाणि देही स्वगुणैर्वृणोति ।
क्रियागुणैरात्मगुणैश्च तेषां संयोगहेतुरपरोऽपि दृष्टः ॥ १२

sthūlāni sūkṣmāṇi bahūni caiva rūpāṇi dehī svaguṇairvṛṇoti |
kriyāguṇairātmaguṇaiśca teṣāṃ saṃyogaheturaparo'pi dṛṣṭaḥ ||
12

5.12 Whether gross or subtle, rich or poor, handsome or ugly, each name and form has many traits that justify its appearance, and some traits that bewilder and cause a wonder.

The soul is able to transform even a coward to a hero of famous exploits, when its body is blessed by the glance of a Master, and when it starts to implement the will of the Master.

The Master is simply a brighter soul, and it can make the dimmest soul qualify for the ultimate.

A current may be weak, and the light may be dull, a body might be mighty and have many powers to support it, but if the Master is missing (like the absence of a soccer coach or a secretary to the minister), then the evolution takes a downward spiral.

Even for such suffering, discarded or wrongly guided souls, the end is the same, dissolution in Brahman.

अनाद्यनन्तं कलिलस्य मध्ये विश्वस्य स्रष्टारमनेकरूपम् ।
विश्वस्यैकं परिवेष्टितारं ज्ञात्वा देवं मुच्यते सर्वपाशैः ॥ १३

anādyanantaṃ kalilasya madhye viśvasya sraṣṭhāramanekarūpam | viśvasyaikaṃ pariveṣṭitāraṃ jñātvā devaṃ mucyate sarvapāśaiḥ || 13

5.13 Can you say who came first, can you pinpoint where time starts and where space ends?

Such unanswered questions are faced by us regularly. We also do not know what our son wants or who our daughter is planning to marry. Nor can we foresee who shall win the election, or who shall be the next genius.

In spite of uncertainty, there is a strong faith 'i am well taken care of'. In spite of chaos, there is a striking beauty in nature. In spite of traffic snarls and long driving times, there is a hope 'i shall make it'.

Who or what is this faith? What is hope? Even the newborn birds, saplings, and little puppies know that they will be looked after. Their needs shall be met. Their desires and longings shall be quenched.

What is there in creation that gives such a guarantee? Who is He that takes the responsibility of events that none can bear? Who ensures that planes and rockets shall land safely? Who fills a mother with love for her newborn?

Do you ever ponder? Do you ever seek? The wise say - the man who embarks on the search for Lord is the one who is the most fortunate.

भावग्राह्यमनीडाख्यं भावाभावकरं शिवम् ।
कलासर्गकरं देवं ये विदुस्ते जहुस्तनुम् ॥ १४

bhāvagrāhyamanīḍākhyaṃ bhāvābhāvakaraṃ śivam |
kalāsargakaraṃ devaṃ ye viduste jahustanum || 14

5.14 He is known as Shiva. The auspicious. श् इ व् आ । श for *shanti* = calmness. इ for *iti* = right now and here. व् for *vishwas* = deep faith. आ for *aang* = all inclusive and all pervasive.

And how to know Him? Through the grace of the Master. Through a light that is stronger and can illuminate Him.

In the inner recesses of the heart which feels a moment of freedom and love. In the corner of the mind that has a moment of silent contemplation.

And by what name to call Him? Devi Durga Radha Ganesha Krishna Nanak Mahavir? Or any other? The Upanishad says 'He answers to all names'. He knows He is being called irrespective of your station or nationality. Irrespective of your language or style of calling.

And how do we know He has heard? Only the heart shall know. His appearance and form cannot be drawn, His manner and personality cannot be stated. But whosoever glimpses Him shall know. His nectar shall remain. His bliss shall light your way.

6th Teaching (leela of Brahman)

The cosmic play of Brahman

षष्ठोऽध्यायः

स्वभावमेके कवयो वदन्ति कालं तथान्ये परिमुह्यमानाः ।

देवस्यैष महिमा तु लोके येनेदं भ्राम्यते ब्रह्मचक्रम् ॥ १

ṣaṣṭho'dhyāyaḥ

svabhāvameke kavayo vadanti kālaṃ tathānye parimuhyamānāḥ |

devasyaiṣa mahimā tu loke yenedaṃ bhrāmyate brahmacakram ॥
1

6.1 The pundits and scholars and academics are divided over the origin and cause of the universe. A large number believe there is independent control of many things and principles, i.e. there are many independent forces that govern the creation.

Then some others are of the view that there is a ruler of time, and that in turn gives life to all particles.

Both have a point, and there is certainly someone Other as well that governs it all. The great Lord whom none can define, yet all can intuitively feel.

The Lord's wheel all experience as a set of ups and downs, as birth and death, as beginning and finishing, as irritating pin pricks or small victories, as waves of doubt or of all is well.

येनावृतं नित्यमिदं हि सर्वं ज्ञः कालकारो गुणी सर्वविद्यः ।
तेनेशितं कर्म विवर्तते ह पृथिव्यप्तेजोंइलखानि चिन्त्यम् ॥ २

yenāvṛtaṃ nityamidaṃ hi sarvaṃ jñaḥ kālakāro guṇī sarvavidyaḥ |
teneśitaṃ karma vivartate ha pṛthivyaptejomilakhāni cintyam || 2

तत्कर्म कृत्वा विनिवर्त्य भूयस्तत्त्वस्य तत्त्वेन समेत्य योगम् ।
एकेन द्वाभ्यां त्रिभिरष्टभिर्वा कालेन चैवात्मगुणैश्च सूक्ष्मैः ॥ ३

tatkarma kṛtvā vinivartya bhūyastattvasya tattvena sametya yogam
| ekena dvābhyāṃ tribhiraṣṭabhirvā kālena caivātmaguṇaiśca
sūkṣmaiḥ || 3

6.2 The Lord's mystery is deepened due to the fact that he is at times, and then he is not within the folds of creation. At one moment He is in the smile of a child, and the next moment He's gone. He is present in some graceful activity, but He never stays for long.

Like the intense passion, the awe of wonder, the deep longing, the final burst to cross the finishing line, all earth-shaking in magnitude but encapsulated in a momentary flash.

The Lord has given each immense free will. There is a large degree of latitude and lots of options, many paths. He is not going to fix anyone's will, nor does He bother to prevent anyone from blunder. He plays a game of "do what you want, it shall affect you alone, for me all is acceptable".

Very hard to digest, impossible to reason out are His ways. At the end of each one's allotted timespan, (400 years for human beings), all merge into Him, all achieve union with Him.

Whether Time, whether Nature, whether an atom of Space, the Lord is present therein, however none of them is the Lord. The Lord prefers to be dormant. Even though present, as if He is not.

It cannot be said He caused an event, yet it is hard to dissociate Him from anything.

He is certainly not the cruel tyrant who is causing hell all around. He is certainly not the stupid moron who is responsible for wastage of natural resources or who causes pollution and emotional upheavel.

Yet can we say He doesn't notice these things? Can we say the ignorant do not derive ignorance by His will?

Some questions cannot so simply be answered. All that can be said is the Lord causes no harm, nor any destruction or any turmoil. The Lord does not stand in the way of anyone's success. The Lord does not cause illness or poverty.

Then does earth make mistakes? Does water choose to become polluted? Does fire cause wilful damage? Does air become unbreathable? And does space run out?

6.3 The answer to the above is rather hazy. One explanation given is that man reaps the fruit of his own sowing. Some men due to bitterness sow terrible seeds that sprout to cause suffering. The Upanishad says the suffering cannot touch the pure. The innocent can never fall prey to wickedness.

Sometimes it may appear that a good man is being abused, however deep inside there are wounds and errors yet unrepented for and brushed aside, so the memory has forgotten its own earlier terrible actions.

The union with the divine is everyone's longing, however when one's actions and attitude do not qualify for the same, then it is impossible that He shall manifest in one's life.

Brahman gives chances, or creates situations for man to evolve. It is noticed that the brave make the grade in the first attempt itself. They are the ones who are hailed as the enlightened masters. For them" soham that is me", this one principle manifests.

The ones with intense passion are next to cross over, and a close third are those who do not give up.

Passion is Bhakti and the second principle after bravery.

Doggedness or purusharth is the third principle that manifests at the middle of the pyramid.

Then we see the devotees and disciples who heed the words of the master and are willing to make a u-turn in life. These ordinary men and women are unnoticed by the media, are present in every town, and make use of one facet of Yoga.

In them, one of the eight cornerstones of Yoga is blossomed. It could be Ahimsa or compassion, it could be asana or body fitness,
It could be pranayama or control of emotions, it could be pratyahara or control of senses, dharana one-pointedness in speech and action, dhyana contemplation on who am i and what is my purpose, or samadhi letting go in total surrender.

आरभ्य कर्माणि गुणान्वितानि भावांश्च सर्वान्विनियोजयेद्यः ।
तेषामभावे कृतकर्मनाशः कर्मक्षये याति स तत्त्वतोऽन्यः ॥ ४

ārabhya karmāṇi guṇānvitāni bhāvāṃśca sarvānviniyojayedyaḥ |
teṣāmabhāve kṛtakarmanāśaḥ karmakṣaye yāti sa tattvato'nyaḥ ||
4

आदिः स संयोगनिमित्तहेतुः परस्त्रिकालादकलोऽपि दृष्टः ।
तं विश्वरूपं भवभूतमीड्यं देवं स्वचित्तस्थमुपास्य पूर्वम् ॥ ५

ādiḥ sa saṃyoganimittahetuḥ parastrikālādakalo'pi dṛṣṭaḥ | taṃ
viśvarūpaṃ bhavabhūtamīḍyaṃ devaṃ svacittasthamupāsya
pūrvam || 5

6.4 In the beginning a child or a disciple is open and accepting, with regard and belongingness for all. Thereafter a particular discipline and master and mode of living takes prominence and undue distractions and time and energy leakages get limited.

This helps preserve the vitality so needed for the smooth journey of a 400 year lifespan, and it also minimizes the moments when one is out of tune with nature.

A day comes when fear and suffering bid final adieu, and nature envelops the devotee in an impregnable force field where fountains of bliss and uninhibited adventures spring.

6.5 Such a devotee glimpses the great Lord, and his gratefulness knows no bounds.

The devotee acknowledges a supreme oneness in creation where a beginning is an ending, where all endings are new beginnings, where cause and effect are strongly intertwined, and each effect is a new cause.

He sees each man as someone's savior, behelds each woman with a beloved, his journey then becomes timeless, ageless, tireless. Time answers to his needs, Time dilates to accomodate his pace, Time ensures his timeliness.

Such a devotee is adored by generations, such a devotee becomes a legend. What he does sets a precedence, what he wishes becomes the wish of the populace.

स वृक्षकालाकृतिभिः परोऽन्यो यस्मात्प्रपञ्चः परिवर्ततेऽयम् ।
धर्मावहं पापनुदं भगेशं ज्ञात्वात्मस्थममृतं विश्वधाम ॥ ६

sa vṛkṣakālākṛtibhiḥ paro'nyo yasmāt prapañcaḥ parivartate'yam |
dharmāvahaṃ pāpanudaṃ bhageśaṃ jñātvātmasthamamṛtaṃ
viśvadhāma ॥ 6

तमीश्वराणां परमं महेश्वरं तं देवतानां परमं च दैवतम् ।
पतिं पतीनां परमं परस्ताद्विदाम देवं भुवनेशमीड्यम् ॥ ७

tamīśvarāṇāṃ paramaṃ maheśvaraṃ taṃ devatānāṃ paramaṃ ca
daivatam | patiṃ patīnāṃ paramaṃ parastād vidāma devaṃ
bhuvaneśamīḍyam ॥ 7

6.6 Such a devotee is protected by trees, acknowledged by phenomena, and shaped by the unknown.

Such a devotee can mix elements and create wonders at will. He can shape the destiny of individuals as well as of nations. He can banish suffering and join broken hearts. He can cause euphoria in families and cities.

We all hope to perceive the brilliant Lord in this small frame, quiet tongue and nondescript appearance.

6.7 The rare one who acknowledges such a devotee, who honors him completely, who sees in him the source, that rare soul transcends the cloud web and crosses over the sea of unending travail.

We are fortunate to be such rare seekers, we are the blessed ones who glimpsed the Lord and touched infinity.

By some unknown coincidence, we saw through the veil. We saw a bar of solid gold-like glow of divinity, a beam of purity and in a flash our intellect bowed with full support of the ego. Our consciousness made way for the big, for the superior, for the vast. Our soul welcomed whole-heartedly the brilliant light, the splendorous magnificence.

न तस्य कार्यं करणं च विद्यते न तत्समश्चाभ्यधिकश्च दृश्यते ।
परास्य शक्तिर्विविधैव श्रूयते स्वाभाविकी ज्ञानबलक्रिया ॥ ८

na tasya kāryaṃ karaṇaṃ ca vidyate na tatsamaścābhyadhikaśca

dṛśyate | parāsya śaktirvividhaiva śrūyate svābhāvikī

jñānabalakriyā || 8

6.8 Not just for a rare devotee, nor just to unusual seeking, the Lord answers to calls which cannot be adequately described, which cannot be logically deduced, which have never been mentioned nor written.

The Lord's workmanship and His class are so well hidden that none except the brave ever attempts or grasps. The Lord's plan and strategy are coded deep into each nuclei, His design blueprint is woven tightly in every fold of space and every instance of time.

Matter transforms to life, energy condenses to matter, thoughts dream and emotions cleave, His signature is not evident to the smartest, His workmanship goes unperceived by the city folk.

The masterly unknown is unremembered while the local lads and supermoms get all the credit. Those who try to talk of Him limit Him severely by their narrow bias, the pundits prattle of Him in metaphors that do not do Him justice.

O who can describe the Undescribable, who can portray Him who creates the sun and the blackhole?

न तस्य कश्चित्पतिरस्ति लोके न चेशिता नैव च तस्य लिङ्गम् ।
स कारणं करणाधिपाधिपो न चास्य कश्चिज्जनिता न चाधिपः ॥ ९

na tasya kaścit patirasti loke na ceśitā naiva ca tasya liṅgam | sa
kāraṇaṃ karaṇādhipādhipo na cāsya kaścijjanitā na cādhipaḥ ॥ 9

6.9 Brahman has the uniqueness of being a husband to both the men and the women. And also to the non-living. Husband here meaning the provider, the taking care, the security, and the guarantee.

Brahman is the entity that causes rulers to function, that makes it appear to the president that he is in charge, that instills a notion in the emperor that his dominion is his.

Brahman doesn't have a fixed shape or form or any characteristic that is clearly identifiable. Brahman is impervious to the senses and beyond any logical or illogical reasoning. Brahman manifests at will in things big or small, beautiful or weird.

Brahman can tune to any wavelength, Brahman can be friends with any temperament.

Brahman is beyond cause and effect. Brahman is the parent and the sibling, the child and the distant relative. Brahman is the ruler and the ruled, Brahman is beyond rules.

यस्तुर्णनाभ इव तन्तुभिः प्रधानजैः स्वभावतः ।
देव एकः स्वमावृणोति स नो दधात्ब्रह्माप्ययम् ॥ १०

yasturṇanābha iva tantubhiḥ pradhānajaiḥ svabhāvataḥ ǀ deva ekaḥ
svamāvṛṇoti sa no dadhātdbrahmāpyayam ǁ 10

एको देवः सर्वभूतेषु गूढः सर्वव्यापी सर्वभूतान्तरात्मा ।
कर्माध्यक्षः सर्वभूताधिवासः साक्षी चेता केवलो निर्गुणश्च ॥ ११

eko devaḥ sarvabhūteṣu gūḍhaḥ sarvavyāpī sarvabhūtāntarātmā ǀ
karmādhyakṣaḥ sarvabhūtādhivāsaḥ sākṣī cetā kevalo nirguṇaśca ǁ
11

6.10 An allegory is painted. A spider and its web is told.

Man uses brick and cement and stuff other than his body and not born of his body to fashion dwellings. He furnishes himself with comforts not produced of his genes.

Brahman doesn't need a dwelling, Brahman is not interested in any production, yet this universe is as if made by Him to suit His taste. The currents and energies are like luminous strands, the forces of nature are like a criss-cross web. O compassionate Brahman! May thee resolve our conflicts and banish our doubts. May thee just in a trice accept us in thy embrace.

6.11 O such wonder! Thee are in us and beside us and ever ready to lend a hand, but our radar cannot identify thy presence and our intellect cannot digest thy variability.

Even most of our involuntary functions are guided and made operational by thee alone.

All our pragmatic efforts bear fruits by thy grace alone. Our healthy emotions are a direct result of your compassion. Our able works and sound judgements stem only due to your attendance.

We hope you preside over our errors and commissions too, though it is clear you are not aware of such occurrences at all. You are no witness to crime and negligence, you are no accomplice to pride and prejudice. Our headaches and heartburns, our lust and infatuation are far far far removed from thy will, thy sight, and thy involvement.

एको वशी निष्क्रियाणां बहूनामेकं बीजं बहुधा यः करोति ।
तमात्मस्थं येऽनुपश्यन्ति धीरास्तेषां सुखं शाश्वतं नेतरेषाम् ॥ १२

eko vaśī niṣkriyāṇāṃ bahūnāmekaṃ bījaṃ bahudhā yaḥ karoti |
tamātmastham ye'nupaśyanti dhīrāsteṣāṃ sukhaṃ śāśvataṃ
netareṣām || 12

6.12 Strolling along alone on the timeSpace motorway, Brahman suddenly boomed, without a thought.

At that time thought currents were absent. In a flash varied thoughts manifested and innumerable things and beings and energies took birth.

It is said one in ten million get to glimpse the Brahman who is behind and below, within, and above and in front of it all. This glimpse is a nectar like force that over time ensures freedom by guiding the path, correcting the imbalances, and charting a course of self-discipline or Yoga.

Freedom from what? From the notion "i am this body and these are my assets and this is my status and purpose", and likewise all other types of (un)limited fancies.

नित्यो नित्यानां चेतनश्चेतनानामेको बहूनां यो विदधाति कामान् ।
तत्कारणं सांख्ययोगाधिगम्यं ज्ञात्वा देवं मुच्यते सर्वपाशैः ॥ १३

nityo nityānāṃ cetanaścetanānāmeko bahūnāṃ yo vidadhāti kāmān
| tatkāraṇaṃ sāṃkhyayogādhigamyaṃ jñātvā devaṃ mucyate
sarvapāśaiḥ ॥ 13

6.13 Have you ever thought, "who or what propels me, inspires me, causes likes and dislikes in me, frustrations or excitements, infuses my vision and mission?"

The Upanishad says there is an imperceptible entity flowing within and pervading the entire space. This entity known as Brahman is not graspable by any means, neither is it certain which thought and what act is Its will.

In most cases, one may directly attribute noble, sacred, benevolent and extraordinary acts to His will. In some cases, harsh and unpleasant acts are also His will, when seen in the context of a larger timeSpace band, while "some good" acts are certainly not His will when seen accordingly.

A fundamental aspect of creation, known as the mathematical principle, and all of the math that governs creation, known as Sankhya or balanced design, is a direct evidence of Brahman or a superior entity that none controls or can interface with, yet that oversees all and remains unaffected and unaltered across eons.

The subtle aspect of creation known as Yoga, which comes into play in human beings and higher beings like bhakta, siddha, gandharva, yaksa, apsara, also aims for Brahman. Yoga and Yogic teachings highlight the universal force and unity inherent in creation, and strive to make man rise above his limited frame or touchy identity and touch infinity.

न तत्र सूर्यो भाति न चन्द्रतारकं नेमा विद्युतो भान्ति कुतोऽयमग्निः ।
तमेव भान्तमनुभाति सर्वं तस्य भासा सर्वमिदं विभाति ॥ १४

na tatra sūryo bhāti na candratārakaṃ nemā vidyuto bhānti
kuto'yamagniḥ | tameva bhāntamanubhāti sarvaṃ tasya bhāsā
sarvamidaṃ vibhāti ‖ 14

6.14 Brahman's aspect is supposed to be far more than the transactable universe.

Apart from blackholes, star clusters, nebulae, quasars; or the principles of gravity, magnetism, acceleration; or fundamental particles like photons and phonons; or the deep emotions of romantic love, Brahman has aspects that are new and newly discovered, that keep getting known bit by bit, and technologies and gadgets that can forever be tweaked and improved upon and invented.

With each successive slice of history, previously unheard of phenomena come to light, some principles become extinct, new ones get created.

Brahman is not limited by men or machines or nature, Brahman is not bound by principles nor by fundamental particles.

No being whether saint or king or scientist or genius or deity can ever gauge the possibilities of Brahman, no principle can ever circumambulate Him.

Brahman is the oil that keeps joints functional, flames lit, and love available. Brahman is the glue that helps join minds, Brahman is the power that powers electric currents, Brahman is the compassion in an innocent heart.

एको हꣳसो भुवनस्यास्य मध्ये स एवाग्निः सलिले संनिविष्टः ।
तमेव विदित्वा अतिमृत्युमेति नान्यः पन्था विद्यतेऽयनाय ॥ १५

eko ha(gum)so bhuvanasyāsya madhye sa evāgniḥ salile
saṃniviṣṭaḥ | tameva viditvā atimṛtyumeti nānyaḥ panthā
vidyate'yanāya || 15

6.15 An allegory is portrayed here. Some characteristics of the bird known as Swan are highlighted as desirable and ideal, pure whiteness, herbivorous, mating for life, protective of family, symbol of glowing light and soothing sound, feathers that remain absolutely dry even though the swan swims.

Mythology also credits a swan to be able to pick out milk molecules from a mixture of milk and water, and the ability to travel to planes where the soul alone can travel.

The unknown and undiscernable Brahman is said to have such desirable properties by depicting a known entity like swan.

A swan spends a large time in water, and gleams like a bright flame in an expanse of blue. This is the quality of Brahman, as if hot fire on a lake, atonce cooling and warming, atonce vertical and flat, atonce dancing and still.

O rare seeker! O ye who can appreciate this! O he who can think what cannot be thought, who has faith in the unknown, who treads far beyond his comfort zone, who revels in the entirety! Only thee qualifies for nirvana, only thee can respect freedom, only thee can stomach absorption in the Divine.

स विश्वकृद्विश्वविदात्मयोनिर्ज्ञः कालकारो गुणी सर्वविद् यः ।
प्रधानक्षेत्रज्ञपतिर्गुणेशः सꣳसारमोक्षस्थितिबन्धहेतुः ॥ १६

sa viśvakṛdviśvavidātmayonirjñaḥ kālakāro guṇī sarvavid yaḥ |
pradhānakṣetrajñapatirguṇeśaḥ sa(guṃ)sāramokṣasthitibandhahetuḥ
|| 16

6.16 He who permeates the fabric of the universe and is within each molecule, can verily be said to be the emperor.

His emperorship is unique and unmatched, since what He wills it happens, what He wills doesn't happen due to His granting of free will, and what He does not will also happens. The beauty is not that all these three possibilities exist simultaneously, but these possibilities exist based on time slices or yuga. In a certain time slice known as Satyug, His will dominates in entirety. In another time slice known as Kalyug His will exhibits all three flavors.

Again in space slices known as loka, these three possibilities coexist or exist independently.

Finally in body constructs known as yoni, these possibilities are seen to both coexist or exist independently. Such is the masterly governance, such is the precise handling, such is His astute emperorship.

Free will can be a good thing in moderation. Indiscipline can be tolerated in certain situations. Both a genius and a dumbo can be the cause of much grief or heavenly happiness or vice versa in separate instances.

One man's meat is another man's poison, a right here is a wrong there, those wedded to each other might both enjoy cool, or might have a mix of hot and cold.

What is seen, perceived and understood from one point of reference can change its entire theory or nature from another plane. There is no end to the magic, miracles are happening in rapid succession, truth triumphs but in the end.

स तन्मयो ह्यमृत ईशसंस्थो ज्ञः सर्वगो भुवनस्यास्य गोप्ता ।
य ईशो अस्य जगतो नित्यमेव नान्यो हेतुर्विद्यत ईशनाय ॥ १७
sa tanmayo hyamṛta īśasaṃstho jñah sarvago bhuvanasyāsya goptā
| ya īśe asya jagato nityameva nānyo heturvidyata īśanāya || 17

17

यो ब्रह्माणं विदधाति पूर्वं यो वै वेदांश्च प्रहिणोति तस्मै ।
तꣳह देवंआत्मबुद्धिप्रकाशं मुमुक्षुर्वै शरणमहं प्रपद्ये ॥१८
yo brahmānam vidadhāti pūrvam yo vai vedāmśca prahiṇoti tasmai
| ta(guṃ)ha devamātmabuddhiprakāśaṃ mumukṣurvai
śaraṇamahaṃ prapadye || 18

निष्कलं निष्क्रियꣳ शान्तं निरवद्यं निरञ्जनम् ।
अमृतस्य परꣳ सेतुं दग्धेन्दनमिवानलम् ॥ १९
niṣkalaṃ niṣkriya(guṃ) śāntaṃ niravadyaṃ nirañjanam | amṛtasya
para(guṃ) setuṃ dagdhendanamivānalam || 19

6.17 His working is entirely a mystery, very deep, hard to fathom, not within the grasp of the intelligent nor the talented.

Nature doesn't ever give up nor lose patience, so do not ever tempt Her no matter how big you become.

6.18-19

All parents give birth to a son, whom they educate to their maximum capacity, then send into the world, hoping for the best.

That brilliant son, whose intellect remains transparent, whose heart remains in sync, who gets the desire for liberation, such is the son whom the parents bow down to.

This son is so simple that he displays an astonishing level of innocence, purity that is a lifetime's effort to maintain, self humbling patience, and extreme bravery.

Such a son crosses the bridge to infinity, having burnt all connections and bindings.

यदा चर्मवदाकाशं वेष्टयिष्यन्ति मानवाः ।
तदा देवमविज्ञाय दुःखस्यान्तो भविष्यति ॥ २०

yadā carmavadākāśam veṣṭayiṣyanti mānavāḥ | tadā
devamavijñāya duḥkhasyānto bhaviṣyati ॥ 20
20

तपःप्रभावाद्देवप्रसादाच्च ब्रह्म ह श्वेताश्वतरोऽथ विद्वान् ।
अत्याश्रमिभ्यः परमं पवित्रं प्रोवाच सम्यगृषिसङ्घजुष्टम् ॥ २१

tapaḥprabhāvāddevaprasādācca brahma ha śvetāśvataro'tha vidvān |
atyāśramibhyaḥ paramam pavitram provāca samyagṛṣisaṅghajuṣṭam
॥ 21

6.20 When a number of such sons shall discover space travel and recount adventures across the galactic plains,

When maidens shall glow and charm heavens with their spotless beauty, making them arch down to shower bliss on their lovers,

Then all those in the vicinity without much effort nor enough merit, too shall glimpse the freedom, and be ferried across due to their proximity.

6.21

One such son who was fair, one such maiden who was dark, both by their complete faith in the Divine and their total acceptance of each other,

Got the showers of love and bliss, got established in divine will.

Their words became nectar to all eager listeners, their story tore away their afflictions,

they were enshrined for ever in the hearts of men.

वेदान्ते परमं गुह्यं पुराकल्पे प्रचोदितम् ।
नाप्रशान्ताय दातव्यं नापुत्रायाशिष्याय वा पुनः ॥ २२

vedānte paramaṃ guhyaṃ purākalpe pracoditam | nāpraśāntāya
dātavyaṃ nāputrāyāśiṣyāya vā punaḥ || 22

यस्य देवे परा भक्तिर्यथा देवे तथा गुरौ ।
तस्यैते कथिता ह्यर्थाः प्रकाशन्ते महात्मनः । प्रकाशन्ते महात्मनः ॥ २३

yasya deve parā bhaktiryathā deve tathā gurau | tasyaite kathitā
hyarthāḥ prakāśante mahātmanaḥ | prakāśante mahātmanaḥ || 23

6.22

The knowledge shared in this Upanishad had already been revealed to men who walked long before,

It cannot be absorbed by the sullen, nor by the wicked son, or by the frivolous daughter.

It cannot be understood nor digested or made use of by any cheat.

6.23

The son whose devotion is profound, who seeks and befriends a living master,

who adores the Master like the Lord making no distinction,

To such a son these words take root, sprout, blossom and bear fruit.

The fruit of eternity, the fruit of bliss,

Yes, this is the nectar that the great Lord grants,

Yes this is the only joy worth seeking.

Verses quoted in Adi Sankara's Bhashyam

In his Bhashyam, Adi Sankara quotes verses from other texts to clarify the meaning better.

Shvetashvatara Verse	Refer verses from other texts
1.1	Similar discussions in other Upanishads, Katha verse 1.2.18, Chandogya 6.11.3, Brihadaranyaka 4.5.14
1.3	(Subsequent Shvetashvatara verse 4.10, Bhagavad Gita 9.10, 14.5, Vishnu Purana 1.2.66, Katha Upanishad 1.2.12, Taittiriya 2.1.1)
1.4	Chandogya Upanishad verse 3.12.6, 6.1.4, 8.2.1
1.5	Prashna Upanishad verse 6.2, Srimad Bhagvatam 9.19.14, Bhagavad Gita 7.4
1.6	Brihadaranyaka Upanishad 1.4.10
1.7	Chandogya 6.1.4, Brihadaranyaka 3.8.8, 4.4.19, Taittiriya 2.4.1, Katha 1.2.14, Kena 1.3, 1.4
1.8	Bhagavad Gita 15.16, 15.17, Yajnavalkya 3.144, Mandukya Karika 3.5, Vishnu Purana 5.17.32, also Yoga Vasistha
1.9	Bhagavad Gita 4.6, Vishnu Purana 6.7.96, Brihadaranyaka 2.5.18, Katha 2.2.9
1.11	Chandogya Upanishad verse 8.21, Prashna 5.5, 5.7, Brihadaranyaka 3.2.11, 4.4.6, Bhagavad Gita 6.10, 6.28, 6.29, 13.28
1.12	Vishnu Purana 6.6.92, Upanishads Katha 2.2.12, Brihadaranyaka 1.4.7, Prashna 5.5, Maha Narayana 24.1
1.16	Kaushitaki Upanishad 3.8, Bhagavad Gita 10.10, Isha 11, Taittiriya 3.2.1, Prashna 1.16
2.2	Brihadaranyaka 4.3.32
2.4	Katha Upanishad 2.3.10
2.6	Bhagavad Gita 10.11
2.7	Chandogya 5.24.3, Bhagavad Gita 4.37

2.9	Bhagavad Gita 6.16
2.15	Brihadaranyaka 1.4.10
3.1	Bhagavad Gita 7.14
3.11	Vishnu Purana 6.5.74
3.17	Brihadaranyaka Upanishad 4.3.7
3.19	Brihadaranyaka Upanishad 3.7.23
4.11	Brihadaranyaka Upanishad 3.7.12
4.15	Brihadaranyaka Upanishad 1.3.28
4.20	Kena Upanishad 1.6
5.2	Brihadaranyaka Upanishad 3.7.3, Shvetashvatara subsequent verse 6.18
5.14	Prashna Upanishad 6.4
6.3	Bhagavad Gita 7.4
6.4	Bhagavad Gita 5.10, 5.11, 9.27, 9.28
6.5	Kaushitaki Upanishad 3.9, Brihadaranyaka 4.4.16
6.6	Katha Upanishad 2.3.1
6.11	Ashtadhyayi of Panini 5.2.91
6.12	Bhagavad Gita 3.27, 3.28, 3.29
6.14	Bhagavad Gita 15.6
6.15	Chandogya Upanishad 5.9.1
6.18	Brihadaranyaka 4.4.21, Muktikopanishad 2.2.5
6.20	Bhagavad Gita 5.15, 5.16, 5.17
6.21	Brihadaranyaka 4.5.6
6.22	Prashna Upanishad 1.2, Chandogya 8.11.3

Etymology of Upanishad

व्युत्पत्ति
Consider Adi Shankaracharya's derivation of the word 'Upanishad' as given in his bhashyam on the Katha Upanishad.

उप + नि + षद् + क्विप् –> उपनिषद्

The Sanskrit root from Dhatupatha 1c - 854, 6c - 1427 षद्ॢ विशरण–गति–अवसादनेषु has the three meanings, namely विशरण = wither, गति = attain, अवसादनं = sit.

In the context of wisdom, we can say
- wither away one's stupidity
- attain liberation
- sit with a conviction

The upasarga उप stands for nearness, closeness.
The upasarga नि stands for delving into, intense.
The pratyaya क्विप् makes a noun, and while joining, it vanishes entirely.

Thus the word 'Upanishad' is formed, and it has the meaning of destroying one's ignorance and granting freedom, when we sit devotedly at the feet of the Master.

Latin Transliteration Chart

International Alphabet of Sanskrit Transliteration (I.A.S.T.)

a	ā	i	ī	u	ū	ṛ	ṝ	ḷ	
अ	आ	इ	ई	उ	ऊ	ऋ	ॠ	ऌ	
						ृ	ॄ	ॢ	
e	ai	o	au	ṃ	m̐	ḥ	Ardha Visarga	oṃ	
ए	ऐ	ओ	औ	◌ं	◌ँ	◌ः	◌	ॐ	
Consonants are shown with vowel 'a= अ' for uttering									
ka	क	ca	च	ṭa	ट	ta	त	pa	प
kha	ख	cha	छ	ṭha	ठ	tha	थ	pha	फ
ga	ग	ja	ज	ḍa	ड	da	द	ba	ब
gha	घ	jha	झ	ḍha	ढ	dha	ध	bha	भ
ṅa	ङ	ña	ञ	ṇa	ण	na	न	ma	म
ya	ra	la	va		ḻa	'			
य	र	ल	व		ळ	ऽ			
				Consonant only					
śa	ṣa	sa	ha		ka	क्अ = क			
श	ष	स	ह		k	क्			

The symbol ꣳ is pronounced as गुं guṃ. It is an ayogavaha अयोगवाह sound seen in Vedic literature due to Sandhi.

Verses for Chanting

Accents used in Sanskrit verses increase the power and flow of the mantras during chanting.

Anudatta ☉= अनुदात्तः = signifies base pitch.

Udatta = उदात्तः = unmarked, standard pitch.

Svarita = स्वरितः = high pitch.

Dirgha Svarita = दीर्घः स्वरितः=high to low to normal pitch (*In the Digital edition ebook this accent is given as simple Svarita due to lack of international font support*).

॥ अथ कृष्ण-यजुर्वेदीय श्वेताश्वतरोपनिषद् ॥

शान्तिपाठः

ॐ सह नाववतु । सह नौ भुनक्तु । सह वीर्यं करवावहै ।

तेजस्वि नावधीतमस्तु मा विद्विषावहै ॥ ॐ शान्तिः शान्तिः शान्तिः ॥

प्रथमोऽध्यायः

हरिः ॐ ब्रह्मवादिनो वदन्ति ।

किं कारणं ब्रह्म कुतः स्म जाता जीवाम केन क्व च सम्प्रतिष्ठाः ।

अधिष्ठिताः केन सुखेतरेषु वर्तामहे ब्रह्मविदो व्यवस्थाम् ॥ १

कालः स्वभावो नियतिर्यदृच्छा भूतानि योनिः पुरुष इति चिन्त्या ।

संयोग एषां न त्वात्मभावादात्माप्यनीशः सुखदुःखहेतोः ॥ २

ते ध्यानयोगानुगता अपश्यन् देवात्मशक्तिं स्वगुणैर्निगूढाम् ।

यः कारणानि निखिलानि तानि कालात्मयुक्तान्यधितिष्ठत्येकः ॥ ३

तमेकनेमिं त्रिवृतं षोडशान्तं शताधारं विंशतिप्रत्यराभिः ।

अष्टकैः षड्भिर्विश्वरूपैकपाशं त्रिमार्गभेदं द्विनिमित्तैकमोहम् ॥ ४

पञ्चस्रोतोम्बुं पञ्चयोन्युग्रवक्रां पञ्चप्राणोर्मिं पञ्चबुद्ध्यादिमूलाम् ।

पञ्चावर्तां पञ्चदुःखौघवेगां पञ्चाशद्भेदां पञ्चपर्वामधीमः ॥ ५

सर्वाजीवे सर्वसंस्थे बृहन्ते अस्मिन् हंसो भ्राम्यते ब्रह्मचक्रे ।
पृथगात्मानं प्रेरितारं च मत्वा जुष्टस्ततस्तेनामृतत्वमेति ॥ ६
उद्गीतमेतत्परमं तु ब्रह्म तस्मिंस्त्रयं सुप्रतिष्ठाऽक्षरं च ।
अत्रान्तरं ब्रह्मविदो विदित्वा लीना ब्रह्मणि तत्परा योनिमुक्ताः ॥ ७
संयुक्तमेतत् क्षरमक्षरं च व्यक्ताव्यक्तं भरते विश्वमीशः ।
अनीशश्चात्मा बध्यते भोक्तृभावाज्ज्ञात्वा देवं मुच्यते सर्वपाशैः ॥ ८
ज्ञाज्ञौ द्वावजावीशनीशावजा ह्येका भोक्तृभोग्यार्थयुक्ता ।
अनन्तश्चात्मा विश्वरूपो ह्यकर्ता त्रयं यदा विन्दते ब्रह्ममेतत् ॥ ९
क्षरं प्रधानममृताक्षरं हरः क्षरात्मानावीशते देव एकः ।
तस्याभिध्यानाद्योजनात्तत्त्वभावात् भूयश्चान्ते विश्वमायानिवृत्तिः ॥ १०
ज्ञात्वा देवं सर्वपाशापहानिः क्षीणैः क्लैशैर्जन्ममृत्युप्रहाणिः ।
तस्याभिध्यानात्तृतीयं देहभेदे विश्वैश्वर्यं केवल आप्तकामः ॥ ११
एतज्ज्ञेयं नित्यमेवात्मसंस्थं नातः परं वेदितव्यं हि किञ्चित् ।
भोक्ता भोग्यं प्रेरितारं च मत्वा सर्वं प्रोक्तं त्रिविधं ब्रह्ममेतत् ॥ १२
वह्नेर्यथा योनिगतस्य मूर्तिर्न दृश्यते नैव च लिङ्गनाशः ।
स भूय एवेन्धनयोनिगृह्यस्तद्वोभयं वै प्रणवेन देहे ॥ १३
स्वदेहमरणिं कृत्वा प्रणवं चोत्तरारणिम् ।
ध्याननिर्मथनाभ्यासादेवं पश्यन्निगूढवत् ॥ १४
तिलेषु तैलं दधनीव सर्पिरापः स्रोतःस्वरणीषु चाग्निः ।
एवमात्मात्मनि गृह्यतेऽसौ सत्येनैनं तपसा योऽनुपश्यति ॥ १५
सर्वव्यापिनमात्मानं क्षीरे सर्पिरिवार्पितम् ।
आत्मविद्यातपोमूलं तद्ब्रह्मोपनिषत् परम् । तद्ब्रह्मोपनिषत् परम् ॥ १६

<u>द्वितीयोऽध्यायः</u>

युञ्जानः प्रथमं मनस्तत्त्वाय सविता धियः ।
अग्नेर्ज्योतिर्निचाय्य पृथिव्या अध्याभरत् ॥ १

युक्तेन मनसा वयं देवस्य सवितुः सवे ।

सुवर्गेयाय शक्त्या ॥ २

युक्त्वाय मनसा देवान् सुवर्यतो धिया दिवम् ।

बृहज्ज्योतिः करिष्यतः सविता प्रसुवाति तान् ॥ ३

युञ्जते मन उत युञ्जते धियो विप्रा विप्रस्य बृहतो विपश्चितः ।

वि होत्रा दधे वयुनाविदेक इन्मही देवस्य सवितुः परिष्टुतिः ॥ ४

युजे वां ब्रह्म पूर्व्यं नमोभिर्विश्लोक एतु पथ्येव सूरेः ।

श्रृण्वन्तु विश्वे अमृतस्य पुत्रा आ ये धामानि दिव्यानि तस्थुः ॥ ५

अग्निर्यत्राभिमथ्यते वायुर्यत्राधिरुध्यते ।

सोमो यत्रातिरिच्यते तत्र सञ्जायते मनः ॥ ६

सवित्रा प्रसवेन जुषेत ब्रह्म पूर्व्यम् ।

तत्र योनिं कृणवसे न हि ते पूर्तमक्षिपत् ॥ ७

त्रिरुन्नतं स्थाप्य समं शरीरं हृदीन्द्रियाणि मनसा सन्निवेश्य ।

ब्रह्मोडुपेन प्रतरेत विद्वान् स्रोतांसि सर्वाणि भयावहानि ॥ ८

प्राणान् प्रपीड्येह संयुक्तचेष्टः क्षीणे प्राणे नासिकयोच्छ्वसीत ।

दुष्टाश्वयुक्तमिव वाहमेनं विद्वान् मनो धारयेताप्रमत्तः ॥ ९

समे शुचौ शर्करावह्निवालुका विवर्जिते शब्दजलाश्रयादिभिः ।

मनोनुकूले न तु चक्षुपीडने गुहानिवाताश्रयणे प्रयोजयेत् ॥ १०

नीहारधूमार्कानिलानलानां खद्योतविद्युत्स्फटिकशशीनाम् ।

एतानि रूपाणि पुरःसराणि ब्रह्मण्यभिव्यक्तिकराणि योगे ॥ ११

पृथ्व्यप्तेजोऽनिलखे समुत्थिते पञ्चात्मके योगगुणे प्रवृत्ते ।

न तस्य रोगो न जरा न मृत्युः प्राप्तस्य योगाग्निमयं शरीरम् ॥ १२

लघुत्वमारोग्यमलोलुपत्वं वर्णप्रसादं स्वरसौष्ठवं च ।

गन्धः शुभो मूत्रपुरीषमल्पं योगप्रवृत्तिं प्रथमां वदन्ति ॥ १३

यथैव बिम्बं मृदयोपलिप्तं तेजोमयं भ्राजते तत् सुधान्तम् ।

तद्वाऽऽत्मतत्त्वं प्रसमीक्ष्य देही एकः कृतार्थो भवते वीतशोकः ॥ १४

यदात्मतत्त्वेन तु ब्रह्मतत्त्वं दीपोपमेनेह युक्तः प्रपश्येत् ।

अजं ध्रुवं सर्वतत्त्वैर्विशुद्धं ज्ञात्वा देवं मुच्यते सर्वपाशैः ॥ १५

एष ह देवः प्रदिशोऽनु सर्वाः पूर्वो ह जातः स उ गर्भे अन्तः ।

स एव जातः स जनिष्यमाणः प्रत्यङ् जनास्तिष्ठति सर्वतोमुखः ॥ १६

यो देवो अग्नौ यो अप्सु यो विश्वं भुवनमाविवेश ।

य ओषधीषु यो वनस्पतिषु तस्मै देवाय नमो नमः ॥ १७

तृतीयोऽध्यायः

य एको जालवानीशत ईशानीभिः सर्वाँल्लोकानीशत ईशनीभिः ।

य एवैक उद्भवे सम्भवे च य एतद्विदुरमृतास्ते भवन्ति ॥ १

एको हि रुद्रो न द्वितीयाय तस्थुर्य इमाँल्लोकानीशत ईशानीभिः ।

प्रत्यङ् जनांस्तिष्ठति सञ्चुकोचान्तकाले संसृज्य विश्वा भुवनानि गोपाः ॥ २

विश्वतश्चक्षुरुत विश्वतोमुखो विश्वतोबाहुरुत विश्वतस्पात् ।

सं बाहुभ्यां धमति संपतत्रैर्द्यावाभूमी जनयन् देव एकः ॥ ३

यो देवानां प्रभवश्चोद्भवश्च विश्वाधिपो रुद्रो महर्षिः ।

हिरण्यगर्भं जनयामास पूर्वं स नो बुद्ध्या शुभया संयुनक्तु ॥ ४

या ते रुद्र शिवा तनूरघोराऽपापकाशिनी ।

तया नस्तनुवा शन्तमया गिरिशन्ताभिचाकशीहि ॥ ५

यामिषुं गिरिशन्त हस्ते बिभर्ष्यस्तवे ।

शिवां गिरित्र तां कुरु मा हिꣲसीः पुरुषं जगत् ॥ ६

ततः परं ब्रह्मपरं बृहन्तं यथानिकायं सर्वभूतेषु गूढम् ।

विश्वस्यैकं परिवेष्टितारमीशं तं ज्ञात्वाऽमृता भवन्ति ॥ ७

वेदाहमेतं पुरुषं महान्तमादित्यवर्णं तमसः परस्तात् ।

तमेव विदित्वाऽतिमृत्युमेति नान्यः पन्था विद्यतेऽयनाय ॥ ८

यस्मात् परं नापरमस्ति किञ्चिद्यस्मान्नाणीयो न ज्यायोऽस्ति कश्चित् ।

वृक्ष इव स्तब्धो दिवि तिष्ठत्येकस्तेनेदं पूर्णं पुरुषेण सर्वम् ॥ ९

ततो यदुत्तरततं तदरूपमनामयम् ।

य एतद्विदुरमृतास्ते भवन्त्यथेतरे दुःखमेवापियन्ति ॥ १०

सर्वाननशिरोग्रीवः सर्वभूतगुहाशयः ।

सर्वव्यापी स भगवांस्तस्मात्सर्वगतः शिवः ॥ ११

महान्प्रभुर्वै पुरुषः सत्वस्यैष प्रवर्तकः ।

सुनिर्मलामिमां प्राप्तिमीशानो ज्योतिरव्ययः ॥ १२

अङ्गुष्ठमात्रः पुरुषोऽन्तरात्मा सदा जनानां हृदये सन्निविष्टः ।

हृदा मन्वीशो मनसाभिक्कृप्तो य एतद्विदुरमृतास्ते भवन्ति ॥ १३

सहस्रशीर्षा पुरुषः सहस्राक्षः सहस्रपात् ।

स भूमिं विश्वतो वृत्वाऽत्यतिष्ठद्दशाङ्गुलम् ॥ १४

पुरुष एवेदꣳ सर्वं यद्भूतं यच्च भव्यम् ।

उतामृतत्वस्येशानो यदन्नेनातिरोहति ॥ १५

सर्वतःपाणिपादं तत् सर्वतोऽक्षिशिरोमुखम् ।

सर्वतः श्रुतिमल्लोके सर्वमावृत्य तिष्ठति ॥ १६

सर्वेन्द्रियगुणाभासं सर्वेन्द्रियविवर्जितम् ।

सर्वस्य प्रभुमीशानं सर्वस्य शरणं बृहत् ॥ १७

नवद्वारे पुरे देही हꣳसो लेलायते बहिः ।

वशी सर्वस्य लोकस्य स्थावरस्य चरस्य च ॥ १८

अपाणिपादो जवनो ग्रहीता पश्यत्यचक्षुः स श‍ृणोत्यकर्णः ।

स वेत्ति वेद्यं न च तस्यास्ति वेत्ता तमाहुरग्र्यं पुरुषं महान्तम् ॥ १९

अणोरणीयान्महतो महीयानात्मा गुहायां निहितोऽस्य जन्तोः ।

तमक्रतुः पश्यति वीतशोको धातुः प्रसादान्महिमानमीशम् ॥ २०

वेदाहमेतमजरं पुराणं सर्वात्मानं सर्वगतं विभुत्वात् ।

जन्मनिरोधं प्रवदन्ति यस्य ब्रह्मवादिनो हि प्रवदन्ति नित्यम् ॥ २१

चतुर्थोऽध्यायः

य एकोऽवर्णो बहुधा शक्तियोगाद्वर्णाननेकान्निहितार्थो दधाति ।
वि चैति चान्ते विश्वमादौ स देवः स नो बुद्ध्या शुभया संयुनक्तु ॥ १

तदेवाग्निस्तदादित्यस्तद्वायुस्तदु चन्द्रमाः ।
तदेव शुक्रं तद्ब्रह्म तदापस्तत्प्रजापतिः ॥ २

त्वं स्त्री त्वं पुमानसि त्वं कुमार उत वा कुमारी ।
त्वं जीर्णो दण्डेन वञ्चसि त्वं जातो भवसि विश्वतोमुखः ॥ ३

नीलः पतङ्गो हरितो लोहिताक्षस्तडिद्गर्भ ऋतवः समुद्राः ।
अनादिमत्त्वं विभुत्वेन वर्तसे यतो जातानि भुवनानि विश्वा ॥ ४

अजामेकां लोहितशुक्लकृष्णां बह्वीः प्रजाः सृजमानां सरूपाः ।
अजो ह्येको जुषमाणोऽनुशेते जहात्येनां भुक्तभोगामजोऽन्यः ॥ ५

द्वा सुपर्णा सयुजा सखाया समानं वृक्षं परिषस्वजाते ।
तयोरन्यः पिप्पलं स्वाद्वत्त्यनश्नन्नन्यो अभिचाकशीति ॥ ६

समाने वृक्षे पुरुषो निमग्नोऽनीशया शोचति मुह्यमानः ।
जुष्टं यदा पश्यत्यन्यमीशमस्य महिमानमिति वीतशोकः ॥ ७

ऋचो अक्षरे परमे व्योमन्यस्मिन्देवा अधि विश्वे निषेदुः ।
यस्तं न वेद किमृचा करिष्यति य इत्तद्विदुस्त इमे समासते ॥ ८

छन्दांसि यज्ञाः क्रतवो व्रतानि भूतं भव्यं यच्च वेदा वदन्ति ।
अस्मान्मायी सृजते विश्वमेतत्तस्मिंश्चान्यो मायया सन्निरुद्धः ॥ ९

मायां तु प्रकृतिं विद्यान्मायिनं च महेश्वरम् ।
तस्यावयवभूतैस्तु व्याप्तं सर्वमिदं जगत् ॥ १०

यो योनिं योनिमधितिष्ठत्येको यस्मिन्निदं सं च वि चैति सर्वम् ।
तमीशानं वरदं देवमीड्यं निचाय्येमां शान्तिमत्यन्तमेति ॥ ११

यो देवानां प्रभवश्चोद्भवश्च विश्वाधिपो रुद्रो महर्षिः ।
हिरण्यगर्भं पश्यत जायमानं स नो बुद्ध्या शुभया संयुनक्तु ॥ १२

यो देवानामधिपो यस्मिँल्लोका अधिश्रिताः ।
य ईशे अस्य द्विपदश्चतुष्पदः कस्मै देवाय हविषा विधेम ॥ १३

सूक्ष्मातिसूक्ष्मं कलिलस्य मध्ये विश्वस्य स्रष्टारमनेकरूपम् ।

विश्वस्यैकं परिवेष्टितारं ज्ञात्वा शिवं शान्तिमत्यन्तमेति ॥ १४

स एव काले भुवनस्य गोप्ता विश्वाधिपः सर्वभूतेषु गूढः ।

यस्मिन्युक्ता ब्रह्मर्षयो देवताश्च तमेवं ज्ञात्वा मृत्युपाशांश्छिनत्ति ॥ १५

घृतात्परं मण्डमिवातिसूक्ष्मं ज्ञात्वा शिवं सर्वभूतेषु गूढम् ।

विश्वस्यैकं परिवेष्टितारं ज्ञात्वा देवं मुच्यते सर्वपाशैः ॥ १६

एष देवो विश्वकर्मा महात्मा सदा जनानां हृदये सन्निविष्टः ।

हृदा मनीषा मनसाभिक्लृप्तो य एतद्विदुरमृतास्ते भवन्ति ॥ १७

यदाऽतमस्तान्न दिवा न रात्रिर्न सन्न चासच्छिव एव केवलः ।

तदक्षरं तत्सवितुर्वरेण्यं प्रज्ञा च तस्मात्प्रसृता पुराणी ॥ १८

नैनमूर्ध्वं न तिर्यञ्चं न मध्ये न परिजग्रभत् ।

न तस्य प्रतिमा अस्ति यस्य नाम महद्यशः ॥ १९

न संदृशे तिष्ठति रूपमस्य न चक्षुषा पश्यति कश्चनैनम् ।

हृदा हृदिस्थं मनसा य एन-मेवं विदुरमृतास्ते भवन्ति ॥ २०

अजात इत्येवं कश्चिद्भीरुः प्रपद्यते ।

रुद्र यत्ते दक्षिणं मुखं तेन मां पाहि नित्यम् ॥ २१

मा नस्तोके तनये मा न आयुषि मा नो गोषु मा न अश्वेषु रीरिषः ।

वीरान् मा नो रुद्र भामितो वधीर्हविष्मन्तः सदामित् त्वा हवामहे ॥ २२

पञ्चमोऽध्यायः

द्वे अक्षरे ब्रह्मपरे त्वनन्ते विद्याविद्ये निहिते यत्र गूढे ।

क्षरं त्वविद्या ह्यमृतं तु विद्या विद्याविद्ये ईशते यस्तु सोऽन्यः ॥ १

यो योनिं योनिमधितिष्ठत्येको विश्वानि रूपाणि योनीश्च सर्वाः ।

ऋषिं प्रसूतं कपिलं यस्तमग्रे ज्ञानैर्बिभर्ति जायमानं च पश्येत् ॥ २

एकैकं जालं बहुधा विकुर्वन्नस्मिन्क्षेत्रे संहरत्येष देवः ।

भूयः सृष्ट्वा पतयस्तथेशः सर्वाधिपत्यं कुरुते महात्मा ॥ ३

सर्वा दिश ऊर्ध्वमधश्च तिर्यक्प्रकाशयन्नाजते यद्वनड्वान् ।
एवं स देवो भगवान्वरेण्यो योनिस्वभावानधितिष्ठत्येकः ॥ ४
यच्च स्वभावं पचति विश्वयोनिः पाच्यांश्च सर्वान्परिणामयेद्यः ।
सर्वमेतद्विश्वमधितिष्ठत्येको गुणांश्च सर्वान्विनियोजयेद् यः ॥ ५
तद्वेदगुह्योपनिषत्सु गूढं तद्ब्रह्मा वेदते ब्रह्मयोनिम् ।
ये पूर्वदेवा ऋषयश्च तद्विदुस्ते तन्मया अमृता वै बभूवुः ॥ ६
गुणान्वयो यः फलकर्मकर्ता कृतस्य तस्यैव स चोपभोक्ता ।
स विश्वरूपस्त्रिगुणस्त्रिवर्त्मा प्राणाधिपः संचरति स्वकर्मभिः ॥ ७
अङ्गुष्ठमात्रो रवितुल्यरूपः सङ्कल्पाहङ्कारसमन्वितो यः ।
बुद्धेर्गुणेनात्मगुणेन चैव आराग्रमात्रो ह्यपरोऽपि दृष्टः ॥ ८
बालाग्रशतभागस्य शतधा कल्पितस्य च ।
भागो जीवः स विज्ञेयः स चानन्त्याय कल्पते ॥ ९
नैव स्त्री न पुमानेष न चैवायं नपुंसकः ।
यद्यच्छरीरमादत्ते तेने तेने स युज्यते ॥ १०
सङ्कल्पनस्पर्शनदृष्टिमोहैर्ग्रासांबुवृष्ट्या चात्मविवृद्धिजन्म ।
कर्मानुगान्यनुक्रमेण देही स्थानेषु रूपाण्यभिसम्प्रपद्यते ॥ ११
स्थूलानि सूक्ष्माणि बहूनि चैव रूपाणि देही स्वगुणैर्वृणोति ।
क्रियागुणैरात्मगुणैश्च तेषां संयोगहेतुरपरोऽपि दृष्टः ॥ १२
अनाद्यनन्तं कलिलस्य मध्ये विश्वस्य स्रष्टारमनेकरूपम् ।
विश्वस्यैकं परिवेष्टितारं ज्ञात्वा देवं मुच्यते सर्वपाशैः ॥ १३
भावग्राह्यमनीडाख्यं भावाभावकरं शिवम् ।
कलासर्गकरं देवं ये विदुस्ते जहुस्तनुम् ॥ १४

षष्ठोऽध्यायः

स्वभावमेके कवयो वदन्ति कालं तथान्ये परिमुह्यमानाः ।
देवस्यैष महिमा तु लोके येनेदं भ्राम्यते ब्रह्मचक्रम् ॥ १

येनावृतं नित्यमिदं हि सर्वं ज्ञः कालकारो गुणी सर्वविद्यः ।
तेनेशितं कर्म विवर्तते ह पृथिव्यप्तेजोऽइलखानि चिन्त्यम् ॥ २

तत्कर्म कृत्वा विनिवर्त्य भूयस्तत्त्वस्य तत्त्वेन समेत्य योगम् ।
एकेन द्वाभ्यां त्रिभिरष्टभिर्वा कालेन चैवात्मगुणैश्च सूक्ष्मैः ॥ ३

आरभ्य कर्माणि गुणान्वितानि भावांश्च सर्वान्विनियोजयेद्यः ।
तेषामभावे कृतकर्मनाशः कर्मक्षये याति स तत्त्वतोऽन्यः ॥ ४

आदिः स संयोगनिमित्तहेतुः परस्त्रिकालादकलोऽपि दृष्टः ।
तं विश्वरूपं भवभूतमीड्यं देवं स्वचित्तस्थमुपास्य पूर्वम् ॥ ५

स वृक्षकालाकृतिभिः परोऽन्यो यस्मात्प्रपञ्चः परिवर्ततेऽयम् ।
धर्मावहं पापनुदं भगेशं ज्ञात्वात्मस्थममृतं विश्वधाम ॥ ६

तमीश्वराणां परमं महेश्वरं तं देवतानां परमं च दैवतम् ।
पतिं पतीनां परमं परस्ताद्विदाम देवं भुवनेशमीड्यम् ॥ ७

न तस्य कार्यं करणं च विद्यते न तत्समश्चाभ्यधिकश्च दृश्यते ।
परास्य शक्तिर्विविधैव श्रूयते स्वाभाविकी ज्ञानबलक्रिया ॥८

न तस्य कश्चित्पतिरस्ति लोके न चेशिता नैव च तस्य लिङ्गम् ।
स कारणं करणाधिपाधिपो न चास्य कश्चिज्जनिता न चाधिपः ॥ ९

यस्तुर्णनाभ इव तन्तुभिः प्रधानजैः स्वभावतः ।
देव एकः स्वमावृणोति स नो दधात्ब्रह्माप्ययम् ॥ १०

एको देवः सर्वभूतेषु गूढः सर्वव्यापी सर्वभूतान्तरात्मा ।
कर्माध्यक्षः सर्वभूताधिवासः साक्षी चेता केवलो निर्गुणश्च ॥ ११

एको वशी निष्क्रियाणां बहूनामेकं बीजं बहुधा यः करोति ।
तमात्मस्थं येऽनुपश्यन्ति धीरास्तेषां सुखं शाश्वतं नेतरेषाम् ॥ १२

नित्यो नित्यानां चेतनश्चेतनानामेको बहूनां यो विदधाति कामान् ।
तत्कारणं सांख्ययोगाधिगम्यं ज्ञात्वा देवं मुच्यते सर्वपाशैः ॥ १३

न तत्र सूर्यो भाति न चन्द्रतारकं नेमा विद्युतो भान्ति कुतोऽयमग्निः ।
तमेव भान्तमनुभाति सर्वं तस्य भासा सर्वमिदं विभाति ॥ १४

एको हꣳसो भुवनस्यास्य मध्ये स एवाग्निः सलिले संनिविष्टः ।
तमेव विदित्वा अतिमृत्युमेति नान्यः पन्था विद्यतेऽयनाय ॥ १५

स विश्वकृद्विश्वविदात्मयोनिर्ज्ञः कालकारो गुणी सर्वविद् यः ।
प्रधानक्षेत्रज्ञपतिर्गुणेशः सꣳसारमोक्षस्थितिबन्धहेतुः ॥ १६

स तन्मयो ह्यमृत ईशसंस्थो ज्ञः सर्वगो भुवनस्यास्य गोप्ता ।
य ईशे अस्य जगतो नित्यमेव नान्यो हेतुर्विद्यत ईशनाय ॥ १७

यो ब्रह्माणं विदधाति पूर्वं यो वै वेदांश्च प्रहिणोति तस्मै ।
तꣳह देवंआत्मबुद्धिप्रकाशं मुमुक्षुर्वै शरणमहं प्रपद्ये ॥ १८

निष्कलं निष्क्रियꣳ शान्तं निरवद्यं निरञ्जनम् ।
अमृतस्य परꣳ सेतुं दग्धेन्दनमिवानलम् ॥ १९

यदा चर्मवदाकाशं वेष्टयिष्यन्ति मानवाः ।
तदा देवमविज्ञाय दुःखस्यान्तो भविष्यति ॥ २०

तपःप्रभावाद्देवप्रसादाच्च ब्रह्म ह श्वेताश्वतरोऽथ विद्वान् ।
अत्याश्रमिभ्यः परमं पवित्रं प्रोवाच सम्यगृषिसङ्घजुष्टम् ॥ २१

वेदान्ते परमं गुह्यं पुराकल्पे प्रचोदितम् ।
नाप्रशान्ताय दातव्यं नापुत्रायाशिष्याय वा पुनः ॥ २२

यस्य देवे परा भक्तिर्यथा देवे तथा गुरौ ।
तस्यैते कथिता ह्यर्थाः प्रकाशान्ते महात्मनः । प्रकाशान्ते महात्मनः ॥ २३

॥ समाप्तमिदं श्वेताश्वतरोपनिषद् ॥

ॐ सह नाववतु । सह नौ भुनक्तु । सह वीर्यं करवावहै ।
तेजस्वि नावधीतमस्तु मा विद्विषावहै ॥ ॐ शान्तिः शान्तिः शान्तिः ॥

|| atha kṛṣṇa-yajurvedīya śvetāśvataropaniṣad ||

śāntipāṭhaḥ

oṃ saha nāvavatu | saha nau bhunaktu | saha vīryaṃ karavāvahai

| tejsvi nāvadhītamastu mā vidviṣāvahai || oṃ śāntiḥ śāntiḥ śāntiḥ

||

prathamo'dhyāyaḥ

hariḥ oṃ brahmavādino vadanti | kiṃ kāraṇaṃ brahma kutaḥ
sma jātā jīvāma kena kva ca sampratiṣṭhāḥ | adhiṣṭhitāḥ kena
sukhetareṣu vartāmahe brahmavido vyavasthām || 1

kālaḥ svabhāvo niyatiryadṛcchā bhūtāni yoniḥ puruṣa iti cintyā |
saṃyoga eṣāṃ na tvātmabhāvādātmāpyanīśaḥ sukhaduḥkhahetoḥ
|| 2

te dhyānayogānugatā apaśyan devātmaśaktiṃ svaguṇairnigūḍhām
| yaḥ kāraṇāni nikhilāni tāni kālātmayuktānyadhitiṣṭhatyekaḥ || 3

tamekanemiṃ trivṛtaṃ ṣoḍaśāntaṃ śatārdhāraṃ
viṃśatipratyarābhiḥ | aṣṭakaiḥ ṣaḍbhirviśvarūpaikapāśaṃ
trimārgabhedaṃ dvinimittaikamoham || 4

pañcasrotombuṃ pañcayonyugravakrāṃ pañcaprāṇormiṃ
pañcabuddhyādimūlām | pañcāvartāṃ pañcaduḥkhaughavegāṃ
pañcāśadbhedāṃ pañcaparvāmadhīmaḥ || 5

sarvājīve sarvasaṃsthe bṛhante asmin haṃso bhrāmyate
brahmacakre | pṛthagātmānaṃ preritāraṃ ca matvā
juṣṭastatastenāmṛtatvameti || 6

udgītametatparamaṃ tu brahma tasmiṃstrayaṃ
supratiṣṭhā'kṣaraṃ ca | atrāntaraṃ brahmavido viditvā līnā
brahmaṇi tatparā yonimuktāḥ || 7

saṃyuktametat kṣaramakṣaraṃ ca vyaktāvyaktaṃ bharate
viśvamīśaḥ | anīśaścātmā badhyate bhoktṛbhāvājjñātvā devaṃ
mucyate sarvapāśaiḥ || 8

jñājñau dvāvajāvīśanīśāvajā hyekā bhoktṛbhogyārthayuktā |
anantaścātmā viśvarūpo hyakartā trayaṃ yadā vindate
brahmametat || 9

kṣaraṃ pradhānamamṛtākṣaraṃ haraḥ kṣarātmānāvīśate deva
ekaḥ | tasyābhidhyānādyojanāttattvabhāvāt bhūyaścānte
viśvamāyānivṛttiḥ || 10

jñātvā devaṃ sarvapāśāpahāniḥ kṣīṇaiḥ

klaiśairjanmamṛtyuprahāṇiḥ | tasyābhidhyānāttṛtīyaṃ dehabhede
viśvaiśvaryaṃ kevala āptakāmaḥ || 11
etajjñeyaṃ nityamevātmasaṃsthaṃ nātaḥ paraṃ veditavyaṃ hi
kiñcit | bhoktā bhogyaṃ preritāraṃ ca matvā sarvaṃ proktaṃ
trividhaṃ brahmametat || 12
vahneryathā yonigatasya mūrtirna dṛśyate naiva ca liṅganāśaḥ |
sa bhūya evendhanayonigṛhyastadvobhayaṃ vai praṇavena dehe
|| 13
svadehamaraṇiṃ kṛtvā praṇavaṃ cottarāraṇim |
dhyānanirmathanābhyāsāddevaṃ paśyannigūḍhavat || 14
tileṣu tailaṃ dadhanīva sarpirāpaḥ srotaḥsvaraṇīṣu cāgniḥ |
evamātmātmani gṛhyate'sau satyenainaṃ tapasā yo'nupaśyati ||15
sarvavyāpinamātmānaṃ kṣīre sarpirivārpitam |
ātmavidyātapomūlaṃ tadbrahmopaniṣat param |
tadbrahmopaniṣat param || 16

dvitīyo'dhyāyaḥ
yuñjānaḥ prathamaṃ manastattvāya savitā dhiyaḥ |
agnerjyotirnicāyya pṛthivyā adhyābharat || 1
yuktena manasā vayaṃ devasya savituḥ save | suvargeyāya śaktyā
|| 2
yuktvāya manasā devān suvaryato dhiyā divam | bṛhajjyotiḥ
kariṣyataḥ savitā prasuvāti tān || 3
yuñjate mana uta yuñjate dhiyo viprā viprasya bṛhato vipaścitaḥ |
vi hotrā dadhe vayunāvideka inmahī devasya savituḥ pariṣṭutiḥ || 4
yuje vāṃ brahma pūrvyaṃ namobhirviśloka etu pathyeva sūreḥ |
śṛṇvantu viśve amṛtasya putrā ā ye dhāmāni divyāni tasthuḥ || 5
agniryatrābhimathyate vāyuryatrādhirudhyate | somo
yatrātiricyate tatra sañjāyate manaḥ || 6

savitrā prasavena juṣeta brahma pūrvyam | tatra yoniṃ kṛṇavase na hi te pūrtamakṣipat || 7

trirunnataṃ sthāpya samaṃ śarīram hṛdīndriyāṇi manasā sanniveśya | brahmoḍupena pratareta vidvān srotāṃsi sarvāṇi bhayāvahāni || 8

prāṇān prapīḍyeha saṃyuktaceṣṭaḥ kṣīṇe prāṇe nāsikayocchvasīta | duṣṭāśvayuktamiva vāhamenaṃ vidvān mano dhārayetāpramattaḥ || 9

same śucau śarkarāvahnivālukā vivarjite śabdajalāśrayādibhiḥ | manonukūle na tu cakṣupīḍane guhānivātāśrayaṇe prayojayet || 10

nīhāradhūmārkānilānalānāṃ khadyotavidyutsphaṭikaśaśīnām | etāni rūpāṇi puraḥsarāṇi brahmaṇyabhivyaktikarāṇi yoge || 11

pṛthvyaptejo'nilakhe samutthite pañcātmake yogaguṇe pravṛtte | na tasya rogo na jarā na mṛtyuḥ prāptasya yogāgnimayaṃ śarīram || 12

laghutvamārogyamalolupatvaṃ varṇaprasādaṃ svarasauṣṭhavaṃ ca | gandhaḥ śubho mūtrapurīṣamalpaṃ yogapravṛttiṃ prathamāṃ vadanti || 13

yathaiva bimbaṃ mṛdayopaliptaṃ tejomayaṃ bhrājate tat sudhāntam | tadvā"tmatattvaṃ prasamīkṣya dehī ekaḥ kṛtārtho bhavate vītaśokaḥ || 14

yadātmatattvena tu brahmatattvaṃ dīpopameneha yuktaḥ prapaśyet | ajaṃ dhruvaṃ sarvatattvairviśuddhaṃ jñātvā devaṃ mucyate sarvapāśaiḥ || 15

eṣa ha devaḥ pradiśo'nu sarvāḥ pūrvo ha jātaḥ sa u garbhe antaḥ | sa eva jātaḥ sa janiṣyamāṇaḥ pratyaṅ janāstiṣṭhati sarvatomukhaḥ || 16

yo devo agnau yo apsu yo viśvaṃ bhuvanamāviveśa | ya oṣadhīṣu yo vanaspatiṣu tasmai devāya namo namaḥ || 17

tṛtīyo'dhyāyaḥ

ya eko jālavānīśata īśanībhiḥ sarvāṁllokānīśata īśanībhiḥ | ya

evaika udbhave sambhave ca ya etadviduramṛtāste bhavanti || 1

eko hi rudro na dvitīyāya tasthurya imāṁllokānīśata īśanībhiḥ |

pratyaṅ janāṁstiṣṭhati sañcukocāntakāle saṃsṛjya viśvā bhuvanāni

gopāḥ || 2

viśvataścakṣuruta viśvatomukho viśvatobāhuruta viśvataspāt |

saṃ bāhubhyāṃ dhamati saṃpatatrairdyāvābhūmī janayan deva

ekaḥ || 3

yo devānāṃ prabhavaścodbhavaśca viśvādhipo rudro maharṣiḥ |

hiraṇyagarbhaṃ janayāmāsa pūrvaṃ sa no buddhyā śubhayā

saṃyunaktu || 4

yā te rudra śivā tanūraghorā'pāpakāśinī | tayā nastanuvā

śantamayā giriśantābhicākaśīhi || 5

yāmiṣuṃ giriśanta haste bibharṣyastave | śivāṃ giritra tāṃ kuru

mā hi(guṃ)sīḥ puruṣaṃ jagat || 6

tataḥ paraṃ brahmaparaṃ bṛhantaṃ yathānikāyaṃ sarvabhūteṣu

gūḍham | viśvasyaikaṃ pariveṣṭitāramīśaṃ taṃ jñātvā'mṛtā

bhavanti || 7

vedāhametaṃ puruṣaṃ mahāntamādityavarṇaṃ tamasaḥ parastāt

| tameva viditvā'timṛtyumeti nānyaḥ panthā vidyate'yanāya || 8

yasmāt paraṃ nāparamasti kiñcidyasmānnāṇīyo na jyāyo'sti kaścit

| vṛkṣa iva stabdho divi tiṣṭhatyekastenedaṃ pūrṇaṃ puruṣeṇa

sarvam || 9

tato yaduttaratataṃ tadarūpamanāmayam | ya

etadviduramṛtāste bhavantyathetare duḥkhamevāpiyanti || 10

sarvānanaśirogrīvaḥ sarvabhūtaguhāśayaḥ | sarvavyāpī sa

bhagavāṃstasmātsarvagataḥ śivaḥ || 11

mahānprabhurvai puruṣaḥ satvasyaiṣa pravartakaḥ |

sunirmalāmimāṃ prāptimīśāno jyotiravyayaḥ || 12

aṅguṣṭhamātraḥ puruṣo'ntarātmā sadā janānāṃ hṛdaye sanniviṣṭaḥ | hṛdā manvīśo manasābhiklṛpto ya etadviduramṛtāste bhavanti || 13

sahasraśīrṣā puruṣaḥ sahasrākṣaḥ sahasrapāt | sa bhūmiṃ viśvato vṛtvā'tyatiṣṭhaddaśāṅgulam || 14

puruṣa eveda(guṃ) sarvaṃ yadbhūtaṃ yacca bhavyam | utāmṛtatvasyeśāno yadannenātirohati || 15

sarvataḥpāṇipādaṃ tat sarvato'kṣiśiromukham | sarvataḥ śrutimalloke sarvamāvṛtya tiṣṭhati || 16

sarvendriyaguṇābhāsaṃ sarvendriyavivarjitam | sarvasya prabhumīśānaṃ sarvasya śaraṇaṃ bṛhat || 17

navadvāre pure dehī ha(guṃ)so lelāyate bahiḥ | vaśī sarvasya lokasya sthāvarasya carasya ca || 18

apāṇipādo javano grahītā paśyatyacakṣuḥ sa śṛṇotyakarṇaḥ | sa vetti vedyaṃ na ca tasyāsti vettā tamāhuragryaṃ puruṣaṃ mahāntam || 19

aṇoraṇīyānmahato mahīyānātmā guhāyāṃ nihito'sya jantoḥ | tamakratuḥ paśyati vītaśoko dhātuḥ prasādānmahimānamīśam ||20

vedāhametamajaraṃ purāṇaṃ sarvātmānaṃ sarvagataṃ vibhutvāt | janmanirodhaṃ pravadanti yasya brahmavādino hi pravadanti nityam || 21

<u>caturtho'dhyāyaḥ</u>

ya eko'varṇo bahudhā śaktiyogādvarṇānanekānnihitārtho dadhāti | vi caiti cānte viśvamādau sa devaḥ sa no buddhyā śubhayā saṃyunaktu || 1

tadevāgnistadādityastadvāyustadu candramāḥ | tadeva śukraṃ tadbrahma tadāpastatprajāpatiḥ || 2

tvaṃ strī tvaṃ pumānasi tvaṃ kumāra uta vā kumārī | tvaṃ jīrṇo daṇḍena vañcasi tvaṃ jāto bhavasi viśvatomukhaḥ || 3 nīlaḥ pataṅgo harito lohitākṣastaḍidgarbha ṛtavaḥ samudrāḥ |

anādimattvaṃ vibhutvena vartase yato jātāni bhuvanāni viśvā || 4

ajāmekāṃ lohitaśuklakṛṣṇāṃ bahvīḥ prajāḥ sṛjamānāṃ sarūpāḥ |

ajo hyeko juṣamāṇo'nuśete jahātyenāṃ bhuktabhogāmajo'nyaḥ ||5

dvā suparṇā sayujā sakhāyā samānaṃ vṛkṣaṃ pariṣasvajāte |

tayoranyaḥ pippalaṃ svādvattyanaśnannanyo abhicākaśīti || 6

samāne vṛkṣe puruṣo nimagno'nīśayā śocati muhyamānaḥ |

juṣṭaṃ yadā paśyatyanyamīśamasya mahimānamiti vītaśokaḥ || 7

ṛco akṣare parame vyomanyasmindevā adhi viśve niṣeduḥ |

yastaṃ na veda kimṛcā kariṣyati ya ittadvidusta ime samāsate || 8

chandāṃsi yajñāḥ kratavo vratāni bhūtaṃ bhavyaṃ yacca vedā

vadanti | asmānmāyī sṛjate viśvametattasmiṃścānyo māyayā

sanniruddhaḥ || 9

māyāṃ tu prakṛtiṃ vidyānmāyinaṃ ca maheśvaram |

tasyāvayavabhūtaistu vyāptaṃ sarvamidaṃ jagat || 10

yo yoniṃ yonimadhitiṣṭhatyeko yasminnidaṃ saṃ ca vi caiti

sarvam | tamīśānaṃ varadaṃ devamīḍyaṃ nicāyyemāṃ

śāntimatyantameti || 11

yo devānāṃ prabhavaścodbhavaśca viśvādhipo rudro maharṣiḥ |

hiraṇyagarbhaṃ paśyata jāyamānaṃ sa no buddhyā śubhayā

saṃyunaktu || 12

yo devānāmadhipo yasmiṃllokā adhiśritāḥ | ya īśe asya

dvipadaścatuṣpadaḥ kasmai devāya haviṣā vidhema || 13

sūkṣmātisūkṣmaṃ kalilasya madhye viśvasya

sraṣṭhāramanekarūpam | viśvasyaikaṃ pariveṣṭitāraṃ jñātvā

śivaṃ śāntimatyantameti || 14

sa eva kāle bhuvanasya goptā viśvādhipaḥ sarvabhūteṣu gūḍhaḥ |

yasminyuktā brahmarṣayo devatāśca tamevaṃ jñātvā

mṛtyupāśāṃśchinatti || 15

ghṛtātparaṃ maṇḍamivātisūkṣmaṃ jñātvā śivaṃ sarvabhūteṣu

gūḍham | viśvasyaikaṃ pariveṣṭitāraṃ jñātvā devaṃ mucyate sarvapāśaiḥ || 16

eṣa devo viśvakarmā mahātmā sadā janānāṃ hṛdaye sanniviṣṭaḥ | hṛdā manīṣā manasābhiklṛpto ya etadviduramṛtāste bhavanti || 17

yadā'tamastānna divā na rātrirna sanna cāsacchiva eva kevalaḥ | tadakṣaraṃ tatsaviturvareṇyaṃ prajñā ca tasmātprasṛtā purāṇī ||18

nainamūrdhvaṃ na tiryañcaṃ na madhye na parijagrabhat | na tasya pratimā asti yasya nāma mahadyaśaḥ || 19

na saṃdṛśe tiṣṭhati rūpamasya na cakṣuṣā paśyati kaścanainam | hṛdā hṛdisthaṃ manasā ya ena-mevaṃ viduramṛtāste bhavanti ||20

ajāta ityevaṃ kaścidbhīruḥ prapadyate | rudra yatte dakṣiṇaṃ mukhaṃ tena māṃ pāhi nityam || 21

mā nastoke tanaye mā na āyuṣi mā no goṣu mā na aśveṣu rīriṣaḥ | vīrān mā no rudra bhāmito vadhīrhaviṣmantaḥ sadāmit tvā havāmahe || 22

pañcamodhyāyaḥ

dve akṣare brahmapare tvanante vidyāvidye nihite yatra gūḍhe | kṣaraṃ tvavidyā hyamṛtaṃ tu vidyā vidyāvidye īśate yastu so'nyaḥ || 1

yo yoniṃ yonimadhitiṣṭhatyeko viśvāni rūpāṇi yonīśca sarvāḥ | ṛṣiṃ prasūtaṃ kapilaṃ yastamagre jñānairbibharti jāyamānaṃ ca paśyet || 2

ekaika jālaṃ bahudhā vikurvannasminkṣetre saṃharatyeṣa devaḥ | bhūyaḥ sṛṣṭvā patayastatheśaḥ sarvādhipatyaṃ kurute mahātmā || 3

sarvā diśa ūrdhvamadhaśca tiryak prakāśayanbhrājate yadvanaḍvān | evaṃ sa devo bhagavānvareṇyo yonisvabhāvānadhitiṣṭhatyekaḥ || 4

yacca svabhāvaṃ pacati viśvayoniḥ pācyāṃśca

sarvānpariṇāmayedyaḥ | sarvametadviśvamadhitiṣṭhatyeko
guṇāṃśca sarvānviniyojayed yaḥ || 5
tadvedaguhyopaniṣatsu gūḍhaṃ tadbrahmā vedate brahmayonim
| ye pūrvaṃdevā ṛṣayaśca tadviduste tanmayā amṛtā vai
babhūvuḥ || 6
guṇānvayo yaḥ phalakarmakartā kṛtasya tasyaiva sa copabhoktā |
sa viśvarūpastriguṇastrivartmā prāṇādhipaḥ saṃcarati
svakarmabhiḥ || 7
aṅguṣṭhamātro ravitulyarūpaḥ saṅkalpāhaṅkārasamanvito yaḥ |
buddherguṇenātmaguṇena caiva ārāgramātro hyaparo'pi dṛṣṭaḥ ||8
bālāgraśatabhāgasya śatadhā kalpitasya ca | bhāgo jīvaḥ sa
vijñeyaḥ sa cānantyāya kalpate || 9
naiva strī na pumāneṣa na caivāyaṃ napuṃsakaḥ |
yadyaccharīramādatte tene tene sa yujyate || 10
saṅkalpanasparśanadṛṣṭimohairgrāsāṃbuvṛṣṭyā
catmavivṛddhijanma | karmānugānyanukrameṇa dehī sthāneṣu
rūpāṇyabhisamprapadyate || 11
sthūlāni sūkṣmāṇi bahūni caiva rūpāṇi dehī svaguṇairvṛṇoti |
kriyāguṇairātmaguṇaiśca teṣāṃ saṃyogaheturaparo'pi dṛṣṭaḥ || 12
anādyanantaṃ kalilasya madhye viśvasya sraṣṭhāramanekarūpam
| viśvasyaikaṃ pariveṣṭitāraṃ jñātvā devaṃ mucyate sarvapāśaiḥ
|| 13
bhāvagrāhyamanīḍākhyaṃ bhāvābhāvakaraṃ śivam |
kalāsargakaraṃ devaṃ ye viduste jahustanum || 14

ṣaṣṭho'dhyāyaḥ
svabhāvameke kavayo vadanti kālaṃ tathānye parimuhyamānāḥ |
devasyaiṣa mahimā tu loke yenedaṃ bhrāmyate brahmacakram ||1
yenāvṛtaṃ nityamidaṃ hi sarvaṃ jñaḥ kālakāro guṇī sarvavidyaḥ |
teneśitaṃ karma vivartate ha pṛthivyaptejomilakhāni cintyam || 2

tatkarma kṛtvā vinivartya bhūyastattvasya tattvena sametya yogam
| ekena dvābhyāṃ tribhiraṣṭabhirvā kālena caivātmaguṇaiśca
sūkṣmaiḥ || 3

ārabhya karmāṇi guṇānvitāni bhāvāṃśca sarvānviniyojayedyaḥ |
teṣāmabhāve kṛtakarmanāśaḥ karmakṣaye yāti sa tattvato'nyaḥ || 4

ādiḥ sa saṃyoganimittahetuḥ parastrikālādakalo'pi dṛṣṭaḥ | taṃ
viśvarūpaṃ bhavabhūtamīḍyaṃ devaṃ svacittasthamupāsya
pūrvam || 5

sa vṛkṣakālākṛtibhiḥ paro'nyo yasmāt prapañcaḥ parivartate'yam |
dharmāvahaṃ pāpanudaṃ bhageśaṃ jñātvātmasthamamṛtaṃ
viśvadhāma || 6

tamīśvarāṇāṃ paramaṃ maheśvaraṃ taṃ devatānāṃ paramaṃ ca
daivatam | patiṃ patīnāṃ paramaṃ parastād vidāma devaṃ
bhuvaneśamīḍyam || 7

na tasya kāryaṃ karaṇaṃ ca vidyate na tatsamaścābhyadhikaśca
dṛśyate | parāsya śaktirvividhaiva śrūyate svābhāvikī
jñānabalakriyā || 8

na tasya kaścit patirasti loke na ceśitā naiva ca tasya liṅgam | sa
kāraṇaṃ karaṇādhipādhipo na cāsya kaścijjanitā na cādhipaḥ || 9

yasturṇanābha iva tantubhiḥ pradhānajaiḥ svabhāvataḥ | deva
ekaḥ svamāvṛṇoti sa no dadhātdbrahmāpyayam || 10

eko devaḥ sarvabhūteṣu gūḍhaḥ sarvavyāpī sarvabhūtāntarātmā |
karmādhyakṣaḥ sarvabhūtādhivāsaḥ sākṣī cetā kevalo nirguṇaśca ||
11

eko vaśī niṣkriyāṇāṃ bahūnāmekaṃ bījaṃ bahudhā yaḥ karoti |
tamātmasthaṃ ye'nupaśyanti dhīrāsteṣāṃ sukhaṃ śāśvataṃ
netareṣām || 12

nityo nityānāṃ cetanaścetanānāmeko bahūnāṃ yo vidadhāti
kāmān | tatkāraṇaṃ sāṃkhyayogādhigamyaṃ jñātvā devaṃ
mucyate sarvapāśaiḥ || 13

na tatra sūryo bhāti na candratārakaṃ nemā vidyuto bhānti
kuto'yamagniḥ | tameva bhāntamanubhāti sarvaṃ tasya bhāsā
sarvamidaṃ vibhāti || 14
eko ha(guṃ)so bhuvanasyāsya madhye sa evāgniḥ salile
saṃniviṣṭaḥ | tameva viditvā atimṛtyumeti nānyaḥ panthā
vidyate'yanāya || 15
sa viśvakṛdviśvavidātmayonirjñaḥ kālakāro guṇī sarvavid yaḥ |
pradhānakṣetrajñapatirguṇeśaḥ
sa(guṃ)sāramokṣasthitibandhahetuḥ || 16
sa tanmayo hyamṛta īśasaṃstho jñaḥ sarvago bhuvanasyāsya goptā
| ya īśe asya jagato nityameva nānyo heturvidyata īśanāya || 17
yo brahmāṇaṃ vidadhāti pūrvaṃ yo vai vedāṃśca prahiṇoti tasmai
| ta(guṃ)ha devamātmabuddhiprakāśaṃ mumukṣurvai
śaraṇamahaṃ prapadye || 18
niṣkalaṃ niṣkriya(guṃ) śāntaṃ niravadyaṃ nirañjanam |
amṛtasya para(guṃ) setuṃ dagdhendanamivānalam || 19
yadā carmavadākāśaṃ veṣṭayiṣyanti mānavāḥ | tadā
devamavijñāya duḥkhasyānto bhaviṣyati || 20
tapaḥprabhāvāddevaprasādācca brahma ha śvetāśvataro'tha
vidvān | atyāśramibhyaḥ paramaṃ pavitraṃ provāca
samyagṛṣisaṅghajuṣṭam || 21
vedānte paramaṃ guhyaṃ purākalpe pracoditam | nāpraśāntāya
dātavyaṃ nāputrāyāśiṣyāya vā punaḥ || 22
yasya deve parā bhaktiryathā deve tathā gurau | tasyaite kathitā
hyarthāḥ prakāśante mahātmanaḥ | prakāśante mahātmanaḥ ||23
|| samāptamidaṃ śvetāśvataropaniṣad ||
oṃ saha nāvavatu | saha nau bhunaktu | saha vīryaṃ karavāvahai
| tejsvi nāvadhītamastu mā vidviṣāvahai || oṃ śāntiḥ śāntiḥ śāntiḥ
||

Sanskrit Grammar

Sandhis separated word by word पदच्छेद (प०),

Verses in prose order अन्वय (अ०),and with विभक्ति Cases.

<u>Abbreviations</u>

Nouns

> **m** masculine, **f** feminine, **n** neuter; **V** vocative
>
> **1/1** = vibhakti case from 1 to 7/number 1 to 3

Indeclinables (uninflected nouns or verbs) **0**

In Sanskrit the **adverbs** are mostly uninflected.

Verbs

> **iii/1** = person i to iii / number 1 to 3
>
> **PPP** = Past Participle Passive = क्त
>
> **PPA** = Past Participle Active = क्तवत्
>
> **PrPA** = PresentParticiple Active = शतृ/ शानच्
>
> **PoPP** = PotentialParticiple Passive = य, तव्य, अनीयर्
> (gerund)
>
> तुमुन् = infinitive, in the sense of "to do"

Anusvara and Makara have been kept as they are in Padacheda, to avoid over work. E.g. इदं should be written as इदम् in Padacheda.

Sanskrit Literature frequently omits the verb – "is". The words भवति, अस्ति etc. are implicit.

E.g. तत्परा योनिमुक्ताः ॥ १.७ = तत्परा योनिमुक्ताः भवन्ति ॥

Since Sanskrit is an inflectional language, the **spelling of the same word** changes as per context or usage. Hence words can be **placed anywhere** in a sentence, as in poetic use, without change in meaning. The matrix shows how.

Verb inflections in Sanskrit – a sample chart

982 गम्‌ गतौ – to go, also in the sense of attainment			
Present Tense Active voice लट्‌ कर्त्तरि प्रयोगः			
Person/no	singular	dual	plural
Third	गच्छति[iii/1]	गच्छतः[iii/2]	गच्छन्ति[iii/3]
Second	गच्छसि[ii/1]	गच्छथः[ii/2]	गच्छथ[ii/3]
First	गच्छामि[i/1]	गच्छावः[i/2]	गच्छामः[i/3]

Noun declensions in Sanskrit – a sample chart

Masculine stem, vowel अending			
(र्‌–आ–म्‌–अ) राम[m] Lord's name			
	singular[1]	dual[2]	plural[3]
1 Doer	रामः[1/1]	रामौ[1/2]	रामाः[1/3]
2 Object	रामम्‌[2/1]	रामौ[2/2]	रामान्‌[2/3]
3 by	रामेण[3/1]	रामाभ्याम्‌[3/2]	रामैः[3/3]
4 for	रामाय[4/1]	रामाभ्याम्‌[4/2]	रामेभ्यः[4/3]
5 from	रामात्‌[5/1]	रामाभ्याम्‌[5/2]	रामेभ्यः[5/3]
6 of	रामस्य[6/1]	रामयोः[6/2]	रामाणाम्‌[6/3]
7 in	रामे[7/1]	रामयोः[7/2]	रामेषु[7/3]
Vocative	हे राम[V/1]	हे रामौ[V/2]	हे रामाः[V/3]

Masculine stem, consonant त् ending		
मरुत्[m] Wind, Breeze, Air		

	singular[1]	dual[2]	plural[3]
1 Doer	मरुत् [1/1]	मरुतौ [1/2]	मरुतः [1/3]
2 Object	मरुतम् [2/1]	मरुतौ [2/2]	मरुतः [2/3]
3 by	मरुता [3/1]	मरुद्भ्याम् [3/2]	मरुद्भिः [3/3]
4 for	मरुते [4/1]	मरुद्भ्याम् [4/2]	मरुद्भ्यः [4/3]
5 from	मरुतः [5/1]	मरुद्भ्याम् [5/2]	मरुद्भ्यः [5/3]
6 of	मरुतः [6/1]	मरुतोः [6/2]	मरुताम् [6/3]
7 in	मरुति [7/1]	मरुतोः [7/2]	मरुत्सु [7/3]
Vocative	हे मरुत् [V/1]	हे मरुतौ [V/2]	हे मरुतः [V/3]

Moods and Tenses in Sanskrit

1	लट्	Present Tense
2	लुङ्	Aorist Past Tense, *before from now onwards*
3	लङ्	Imperfect Past Tense – *before from yesterday onwards*
4	लिट्	Perfect Past Tense – *distant unseen past*
5	लृट्	Simple Future Tense – *now onwards*
6	लुट्	Periphrastic Future Tense – *tomorrow onwards*
7	लृङ्	Conditional Mood - *if/then in past or future*
8	लोट्	Imperative Mood – *request*
9	विधि–लिङ्	Potential Mood – *order* विधिलिङ् (also known as Optative Mood)
10	आशीर्–लिङ्	Benedictive Mood – *blessing* आशीर्लिङ् (also used in the sense of a curse)

Conjugation process of Verb

वदन्ति = they say, they describe.

1st conjugation Root, Parasmaipadi.

1009 √ वदँ व्यक्तायां वाचि । to tell, relate, describe.

1.3.1 भूवादयो धातवः । वदँ = वद्अँ ।

1.3.2 उपदेशोऽजनुनासिक इत् । 1.3.9 तस्य लोपः । वद् ।

3.4.69 लः कर्मणि च भावे चाकर्मकेभ्यः । वद् ।

3.2.123 वर्तमाने लट् । 3.4.77 लस्य । वद् + लँट् ।

1.3.3 हलन्त्यम् । 1.3.9 तस्य लोपः । वद्+लँ ।

1.3.2 उपदेशोऽजनुनासिक इत् । 1.3.9तस्य लोपः । वद्+ल ।

3.4.78 तिप्तस्झिसिप्थस्थमिब्वस्मस् तातांझथासाथांध्वमिड्वहिमहिङ् ।

1.4.199 लः परस्मैपदम् । choose Parasmaipada affix.

वद्+झि । we are conjugating third person

1.4.101 तिङस्त्रीणि त्रीणि प्रथममध्यमोत्तमाः ।

1.4.102 तान्येकवचनद्विवचनबहुवचनान्येकशः । वद्+झि । plural

1.4.108 शेषे प्रथमः । वद्+झि । this is called "प्रथमः" i.e. the **first and most** used in language, third person.

3.4.113 तिङ्शित्सार्वधातुकम् । वद्+झि ।

3.1.68 कर्त्तरि शप् । वद्+शप्+झि ।

3.4.113तिङ्शित्सार्वधातुकम् । वद्+शप्+झि ।

7.1.3 झोऽन्तः । वद्+शप्+ अन्ति ।

1.3.3 हलन्त्यम्। 1.3.8लशक्वतद्धिते। 1.3.9तस्य लोपः।वद्+अ+अन्ति ।

6.1.97 अतो गुणे । वद्+अन्ति । sandhi drops the अकारः ।

8.3.24 नश्चापदान्तस्य झलि । वद् + अंति । Anusvara appears

8.4.58 अनुस्वारस्य ययि परसवर्णः । वद् + अन्ति ।

Anusvara again changes to नकारः ।

वद् + अन्ति = वदन्ति $^{iii/3}$ लट् । iii = 3rd person, 3 = plural.

Third person plural, Present Tense.

Declension process of Noun

ब्रह्म = Brahma. The Lord. Highest Intelligence.

Stem Brahman ब्रह्मन् n → ब्रह्म neuter Nominative $^{1/1}$

The Great Lord. The Invisible presence.

1.2.45 अर्थवदधातुरप्रत्ययः प्रातिपदिकम् । ब्रह्मन्

1.2.46 कृत्तद्धितसमासाश्च । 3.1.1 प्रत्ययः । 3.1.2 परश्च ।

4.1.1 ङ्याप्प्रातिपदिकात् । 4.1.2 स्वौजस-

मौट्छष्टाभ्याम्भिस्ङेभ्याम्भ्यस्ङसिभ्याम्भ्यस्ङसोसाम्ङ्योस्सुप् ।

1.4.104 विभक्तिश्च । 1.4.103 सुपः = use one of these vibhakti

suffix. ब्रह्मन् + सुँ ।

1.4.22 द्व्येकयोर्द्विवचनैकवचने = singular number taken.

ब्रह्मन् + सुँ ।

7.1.23 स्वमोर्नपुंसकात् । 2.4.13 यस्मात्प्रत्ययविधिस्तदादि प्रत्ययेऽङ्गम् ।

6.4.1 अङ्गस्य । 1st and 2nd case Vibhakti drops for neuter

stem. ब्रह्मन् ।

1.4.17 स्वादिष्वसर्वनामस्थाने । The word gets पदसंज्ञा ।

ब्रह्मन् ।

8.2.7 न लोपः प्रातिपदिकान्तस्य । Final नकार drops.

ब्रह्म $^{n1/1}$ ।

Neuter. First case nominative singular. **Brahma.**
The Highest. The Supreme. Shiva. Purusha. Tao.
The Beautiful, The Love, The Infinite, The Divine.
Any name is **Him.**
All directions point to **It.** Every form is **She.**

References

https://www.ashtangayoga.info/philosophy/sanskrit-and-devanagari/transliteration-tool/

https://www.learnsanskrit.cc/ http://sanskrit.segal.net.br/
https://upanishads.org.in/
https://ashtadhyayi.com/dhatu/

Audio Chant
https://gaana.com/album/shvetashvatara-upanishad

Guided Meditations Sri Sri Ravi Shankar
https://www.youtube.com/watch?v=ECHxnCJYrpM
https://www.youtube.com/watch?v=vzzWLZb4a4g

Swami Tyagisananda – Svetasvataropanisad – 1st – 1949 – Sri Ramakrishna Math, Mylapore Madras.

Swami Nikhilananda – The Upanishads Vol II – 1st – 1952 – Harper & Brothers Publishers, New York.

Gita Press – श्वेताश्वतरोपनिषद् सानुवाद शाङ्करभाष्यसहित – 1st - 1995 – Gita Press, Gorakhpur.

Swami Devarupananda – मन्त्रपुष्पम् - 4th – 2010 – Ramakrishna Math, Khar, Mumbai.

Ashwini Kumar Aggarwal
    – Dhatupatha of Panini – 2nd – 2017 –
    – Sanskrit Sandhi Handbook – 1st – 2019 –
    – Sanskrit Nouns Sabda Manjari – 1st – 2019 –
Devotees of Sri Sri Ravi Shankar Ashram, Punjab.

Epilogue

White or Non-White, Man's inner color is both and neither.
White light splits into seven colors of a rainbow to indicate
the seven continents and seven oceans, i.e. all of humanity.
Black or Dark hair is as attractive as red or blonde.

Take your pick, someday you shall know Two as One.

सर्वे भवन्तु सुखिनः । सर्वे सन्तु निरामयाः ।

सर्वे भद्राणि पश्यन्तु । मा कश्चिद् दुःख भाग्भवेत् ॥

ॐ शान्तिः शान्तिः शान्तिः ॥

When faith has blossomed in life,
Every step is led by the Divine.

Sri Sri Ravi Shankar

Om Namah Shivaya

जय गुरुदेव